Better After the Battle

Finding God's Strength to Overcome Turbulent Times

Karen Brown Tyson

Constant Communicators, LLC

BETTER AFTER THE BATTLE

To the memories of Edna Brown and Jeffie Jackson
To Kelvin for always being by my side
and to my young prince, Cole, thank you for being a mighty warrior
for God.

Contents

Chapter One

Facing The Fight

Be clearheaded. Keep alert.
Your accuser, the devil, is
on the prowl like a roaring
lion, seeking someone to de-
vour.
–1 Peter 5:8 CEB

With tears running down my face, I sat on the examining table in disbelief. The brightest light in the dimly lit room came from the monitor used to find the tumors in my body. One was in my right breast, and the other under my right arm.

The doctor who performed my biopsy stood behind me and said, "I'm afraid that what we're looking at is cancer."

Although my biopsy results would not be back until Tuesday, she said she didn't think it would be right to have me wait in suspense for three days until she delivered her diagnosis. She thought it would be better to rip the Band-Aid off quickly. Ouch!

After my biopsy, I was scheduled to get another mammogram. The room wasn't ready, so I stayed in the examination room. Sitting there, I kept thinking, 'I don't want this. I don't want cancer.' Not because I didn't think I would be there or because no one in my family had breast cancer. I just didn't want to go through cancer. I didn't want to give cancer the time or the energy it demands.

The first thing I thought about was God's promise, "Never will I leave you; never will I forsake you." It was a promise from God that I relied on in the past. Here I was, wondering if I could count on Him again. Of course, I could. Deep down inside, I knew that no matter what happened, God would be with me every step of the way.

Trusting God is important in a society that promotes self-reliance and entitlement. Once I gave my life to Christ at age 16, I had to acknowledge my identity and belonging to Him. Throughout my life, God has been faithful in providing the strength and hope I need to get through difficult times. I knew from experience that God would be there to protect and guide me through my newest battle.

The next thing I thought about was what would happen next. My first impulse was to fear the unknown. My head was spinning. I had an overwhelming feeling of helplessness. How would I get through this? In fact, I wondered how I would get out of that examination room. But, at that moment, I remembered 1 Peter 5:8:

Be clearheaded. Keep alert. Your accuser, the devil, is on the prowl like a roaring lion, seeking someone to devour.

I knew that the devil was coming for me.

And, if I wanted to get out of that room and be victorious on my cancer journey, I needed to pray. So, I prayed right there on the examination table.

Dear Lord,

I come to you with a grateful heart for exposing these cancer cells early. But I must be honest with you; I don't like this. I don't want cancer. I don't understand what's happening right now. I don't know what to do. But I know you do because you always have a plan. Please give me the strength and courage to get through whatever comes my way. Guide me every step of the way, and let your love and peace surround me.

In Jesus' name, Amen.

I was dazed and confused when I finally left the doctor's office. I felt like I had been hit by a Mack truck.

My husband was finishing a call when I got in the car. *Should I tell him what the doctor said?* My first inclination was to wait until the test results came back. But he is my rock. I had to tell him right away. If anyone could stand to have a Band-Aid-ripping-off-moment, it was him.

He suggested that we go to lunch before returning home. For a while, we drove in silence. Before I knew it, we were at my favorite Chinese restaurant. Once we were seated, I finally blurted out the bad news. As I tried to explain what the doctor told me, I couldn't help but notice how calm he was. He assured me everything would work according to God's plan.

Before I knew it, my husband gave me one of his motivational pep talks, where he told me I could do all things through Christ. He reminded me that I could look to the hills for help and that I could trust God for strength. And in true Kelvin fashion, he told me we would get through this trial together. He ended our little talk by thanking me for being so brave.

But I didn't feel brave. I felt unprepared.

WE ARE AT WAR

We all face tough times in our lives. Regardless of race, gender, or socio-economic status, struggles, trials, and battles will come. At one point in my life, I felt defeated by this simple truth. Not only did I not like facing tough times, but I didn't understand why I even had to go through a trial in the first place. Why me? Why does my life have to be disrupted by this trial? Why can't I just live a trouble-free life? This line of questioning went on in my mind for years. Until the Holy Spirit encouraged me to examine the nature of battles, not just in my life but in the lives of God's people. I discovered at least **five** interesting points that changed my perspective.

Point #1 – Satan has been fighting God since the beginning

God doesn't share ownership. So, when Satan said he would be like God Most High, he was forced to leave heaven (Isaiah 14:12-15 and Revelation 9:1). He was thrown to earth, along with the fallen angels who decided to join him. Since then, Satan has been working to deceive the whole world. Not just you or me, but the *whole* world. He uses deception to influence our thinking through spiritual and worldly means. Now, I will be the first to admit that there have been times when I allowed the enemy to win because I foolishly acted on his deception. But I am learning to reject his lies.

In addition to his commitment to deception, Satan is the accuser of believers. Despite being thrown out of heaven, Satan still has access to God and accuses believers day and night. Satan knows the righteousness of God's character and that human sin breaks fellowship with God. And even if he can't prevent us from being saved, he definitely wants to steal the joy that comes from walking in fellowship with God. So how are we supposed to conquer Satan in our lives? By the blood of the Lamb and the word of our testimony. (Rev. 12:11)

Point #2 – Battles begin in heavenly places

In Ephesians 6:12, Paul reminds us that our battle is not against the people around us, like our coworkers, spouses, bosses, or family members, nor is it against our weaknesses. Our battle is against the rulers, powers, and world forces of wickedness in heavenly places, which refers to the spiritual realm. People only act as conduits of spiritual battles taking place in the spiritual realm.

You know, there's always a spiritual root behind every trial, setback, physical disturbance, ailment, or issue we face. For this reason, Satan will do everything he can to distract us from focusing on the spiritual realm. He works overtime to divert our attention to the people and things we can see, so he can keep us from dealing with the root of the battle, which lies in the spiritual realm.

Point #3 – Not every battle comes from hell

Before we get too far, I want to clarify that every trial or tribulation does not come from hell. We also experience storms and challenges due to natural disasters, our actions, or someone else's choices. In any case, God may allow a battle to come into our lives to uncover sins, develop our character, or teach us how to trust Him no matter what's going on in our lives.

The point is that when our faith is tested, we can grow to become who God wants us to be.

Point #4 – Jesus fought battles of His own

Jesus came from heaven to earth to seek and save the lost (Luke 19:10). He was clear that He didn't come to earth to condemn but rather to bring salvation to all who are open to receiving Him. His ultimate mission was to rescue you, me, and all of humanity from our sins.

But everyone didn't receive Jesus. Everyone didn't like Jesus. Everyone didn't accept Jesus. As a result, Jesus tells His disciples, "If the world hates you, keep in mind that it hated me first." (John 15:18). So, if our battles start in the spiritual realm, and people are used as conduits in our spiritual battles, we can become distracted by the trials and troubles we experience in the physical realm. It's part of Satan's deceptive plan to keep us distracted and frustrated by the people around us rather than staying connected to God through prayer, praise, and fellowship.

Point #5 – Battles build Christian character

It took me a long time to realize that God has some amazing tools that He uses to equip His people for life and service, and believe it or not, suffering is one of them. Peter wrote about the need for trials that extend to all Christians in his letter to the believers scattered throughout Pontus, Galatia, Cappadocia, Asia, and Bithynia. Not only are our trials for a little while but the trials every believer experiences are designed to test our faith.

So, here's the thing: our faith isn't tested because God is clueless about how much or what kind of faith we possess. It's put to the test because *we often have no idea ourselves*. Think about it: Do you really know how much or what kind of faith you have until you have to put your faith into action? The purpose behind God allowing tests and trials to come into our lives is to allow us to develop and showcase the strength of our faith.

Now I understand that as long as I live and breathe, I will face battles occasionally. Will there be good times? Yes. Will there be tough times? Yes. Will joy come in the morning? Yes. Will I win in the end? Absolutely!

So, what battle are you facing? I only ask because I've heard that we are either coming out of a storm, in a storm, or going into a storm. No matter what category you fall into, it's obvious that you started reading this book because you wanted to learn how to deal with the trials in your life. I'm glad you did. Satan doesn't want you to know how to face the challenges in your life. If he had his way, you would take on a defeated mindset, believe his lies, and walk away from your relationship with God.

But my prayer for you is that you will draw close to God through prayer, fellowship, and His word. Because when you do those things, you will find hope in the Lord.

LESSONS FROM SCRIPTURE: Deborah and Barak

Have you ever found yourself walking away from something you know is good for you? That's exactly what Israel did when they turned their backs on God. (Judges 4) As a result, they were handed over to King Jabin of Canaan and oppressed for two decades. But after all that time, they finally realized their mistake and cried out to the Lord for help. It's a powerful reminder that God should be our first call.

Deborah was an extraordinary woman God chose to guide Israel during a challenging time. As a prophetess and judge, she had a direct line to God and could communicate His desires to the people. In particular, Deborah played a critical role in preparing Israel for an upcoming military battle. God spoke through her to call upon a man who would lead the forces to victory. Her inspiring story is a testament to the power of faith and serves as a reminder that God can work through anyone, regardless of gender.

Deborah called upon Barak, a man from Kedesh in Naphtali, to lead the Israelite army against Jabin's forces, led by Sisera. Deborah recognized the need for Israel to be spiritually freed from their social hardships, which would ultimately require a battle to achieve. God revealed His plan and instructions to Barak through Deborah. The Lord declared, "I will lead them to the Kishon River, where you will triumph over them." Barak agreed to the mission, but only on the condition that Deborah accompanied him.

Check out Barak's reluctance when he spoke to Deborah. Although he was talking to Deborah, his response to God's request was, "I'm not going anywhere unless Deborah accompanies me." (v.8). Let's not judge Barak too harshly. How many times has God asked you (and me) to do something, and we hesitated? I cannot tell you how many times I didn't listen to the voice of God.

Here's how Deborah responded, "Of course, I'll go with you. But understand that with an attitude like that, there'll be no glory in it for you. God will use a woman's hand to take care of Sisera." (v.9) On the day of battle, Sisera, Jabin's commander, had 900 chariots lined up to take on Barak and his 10,000 soldiers. Deborah told Barak, "Go! This is the day the Lord has given Sisera into your hands. Has not the Lord gone ahead of you?" (v. 14). Simply put, she told him, "The victory is within your reach, Barak, but you must pursue it." Deborah was right because God put panic in the chariots and troops, allowing Sisera's entire army to be killed.

Sisera ran to Jael's tent as there was an alliance between Jabin, king of Hazor, and Heber, the Kenite. Jael welcomed him and served him warm milk and a blanket. Sisera told Jael to stand guard at the entrance to the tent and lie to anyone who came looking for him. Jael knew that Sisera and Jabin were wicked enemies of God's people. Knowing what was at stake, Jael lured Sisera into a false sense of security. While sleeping, Jael seized the opportunity and hammered a tent peg into his temple, ending his life. Jael will always be remembered as a hero who acted on God's behalf. By the time Barak arrived, Sisera was dead. Deborah's prophesy came true as Jael was credited for ending Sisera's life.

Deborah showed me what it meant to have faith when faced with an impossible challenge. But the truth is that nothing is impossible with God on your side, no matter what you are facing! So, while I didn't exactly lead a battalion into war as Deborah did, her example inspired me. It reminded me that even though cancer seemed like an unbeatable foe, I still could win this battle by leaning on God every step of the way.

YOU DON'T HAVE TO FIGHT ALONE

Life is full of ups and downs, and sometimes we find ourselves in a battle that feels impossible to win. We may feel powerless and alone, wondering how to get through it all. In these moments, the enemy wants us to think we're all alone in our struggles. But the truth is, we don't have to fight alone. God is with us every step of the way. Trusting in God can give you the strength and hope to overcome any challenge.

God promises never to leave or forsake us

One of the most comforting promises that God gives us is that He will never leave or forsake us. Hebrews 13:5 says, "Never will I leave you; never will I forsake you." When we go through tough times, it's easy to feel like we're all alone. But when we remember that God is always with us, we can find peace in the storm.

God is the source of all strength and hope

When we are facing a challenge, it can be difficult to stay strong and positive. That's why it's important to remember that God is the source of all our strength and hope. Isaiah 40:29-30 says, "He gives power to the weak and strength to the powerless. Even youths will become weak and tired, and young men will fall into exhaustion. But those who trust in the Lord will find new strength. They will soar high on wings like eagles. They will run and not grow weary. They will walk and not faint." This verse reminds us that no matter how tough the challenge if we look to God for strength, He will give us the power and courage we need. When life gets tough, we must remember, "Be strong and courageous. Do not be afraid or discouraged."(Deuteronomy 31:6).

Trusting in God is important

Trusting in God is not always easy, but it is essential to find strength in Him. Proverbs 3:5-6 says, "Trust in the Lord with all your heart and lean not on your own understanding; in all your ways submit to him, and he will make your paths straight." When we trust in God, we acknowledge He is in control and has our best interests at heart. We can find rest and peace knowing that He is always with us.

Cancer would be part of my story whether I liked it or not. As I started thinking about the future and what to do next, I had to decide how to face the days and months ahead. Part of me wanted to run, while the other part wanted to give my newfound problem to God. Since the fighter in me wouldn't quit, I moved forward, not knowing what the future held.

Chapter Two

No More Running

Be on your guard; stand
firm in the faith; be coura-
geous; be strong.
-1 Corinthians 16:13 NIV

T he man anxiously paced the wooden floor of his log cabin. He worried about his wife because he had never seen her this sick. Knowing she wouldn't hold on much longer if he didn't do something, he sighed. The year was 1870, and he knew he would have to travel to the next town to get medicine for her. There was only one problem. The only doctor with medicine was on the other side of the lake. Since it was winter, the lake was frozen. Before starting his journey, the man wondered if the lake was safe to cross.

He prayed for guidance and strength, but he was still worried. Before leaving the house, he kissed his wife's forehead. After walking for a few minutes, he reached the edge of the frozen lake. He cautiously stepped onto the ice. He was terrified. So he got down on his hands and knees to crawl across the lake. He moved along slowly. Despite the crisp January air, sweat ran down the man's face. He worried that not only would he not make it to the other side of the lake, but he feared he would never see his wife again.

Suddenly, the man felt a rumbling on the ice. He stopped moving to examine the ice. He didn't see any cracks. He slowly started to crawl forward. When he did, he felt the rumbling again. Maybe the ice is breaking, he thought. As the rumbling sound got louder, he looked behind him and saw a man driving a team of horses across the frozen lake. The horses were pulling a carriage filled with boxes of supplies. The man watched the horses race across the ice uninhibited, without a care in the world.

Slowly, the man stood up and started to walk across the ice. If the frozen lake could hold a team of horses and a carriage full of boxes, it could hold him too. With this new revelation, the man's walking turned into running. Not only did God hear his prayer, but He sent a sign. The man who started his journey full of fear was now a man full of confidence. No longer bound by fear, the man ran to the doctor's office. On his way home, he crossed the ice believing he would make it to the other side.

Once upon a time, you may have felt like that man crossing the ice. I know I have. That's what fear of the unknown will do to you. It will paralyze you to the point that you are so afraid to move forward that you become discouraged or want to give up. When confronted with a battle, the devil often magnifies our fears to the point they appear impossible. He wants to scare us and make us feel uneasy. Once we give in to fear, we become paralyzed and anxious. The reason for this is simple: Fear is one of Satan's primary strategies for hurting God's people. Consider this - the more he can keep us running in circles, the more he can keep us from following God's will.

But like the man on the ice, you can start on your knees. God loves to hear from you in prayer. Ask God to help you overcome the fear of worry, rejection, disappointment, or failure to reach the other side. I want you to decide to run with purpose toward your destiny from this day forward. Like you, I've already decided to stop living life on the run.

> Be on your guard; stand
> firm in the faith; be coura-
> geous; be strong.
> -1 Corinthians 16:13

LESSONS FROM SCRIPTURE: Elijah On the Run

It all happened overnight. One day, Elijah was issuing a challenge at Mount Carmel; the next day, he couldn't get out of town fast enough. One day, he prayed for God to be glorified and the people of Israel edified; the next day, he wouldn't even pray for himself. One day, he was on a spiritual mountaintop; the next day, he was in the valley of the shadow of death.

Talk about going from day to night.

What changed? Jezebel put a hit out on Elijah. The witch queen Jezebel sent Elijah this warning: "You killed my prophets. Now I'm going to kill you! I pray that the gods will punish me even more severely if I don't do it by this time tomorrow." (1 Kings 19:2). So, Elijah became afraid immediately and decided to run for his life.

This was quite a change from the previous chapter. In 1 Kings 18, Elijah challenged all of Israel to meet him at Mount Carmel, including the 450 prophets of Baal and the 400 prophets of Asherah (1 Kings 18:19). Once everyone gathered, Elijah asked, "How long are you going to sit on the fence? If God is the real God, follow him; if it's Baal, follow him. Make up your mind!" (1 Kings 18:21) Elijah's message was clear for everyone at Mount Carmel and present-day believers - you can't have God and the world.

In the end, everyone at Mount Carmel witnessed the following:

- The false prophets called on Baal but received no answer;

- The false prophets danced around the altar, shouted, and cut themselves but received no answer;

- Elijah prepared the altar with stones, dug a wide trench, laid firewood on the altar, and asked that the altar, the ox, and the firewood be drenched with water; and

- Elijah prayed, and fire fell from heaven immediately.

The whole point of Elijah's challenge at Mount Carmel was not to show off. The point was to show the people that the Lord is God. Once the greatness and uniqueness of the Lord had been vindicated and confessed, it was time to dispel the drought and famine from the land. Elijah conveyed to Ahab that a rainstorm was coming and proceeded to the summit of Carmel to pray. With unwavering tenacity, Elijah persisted in intercession until the Lord's answer came pouring down from the heavens. Gifted with supernatural strength, Elijah outran Ahab's chariot as he made his way to Jezreel.

So, what happened? You would think that Elijah would be fearless against a godless Jezebel. Instead, Elijah was seized by fear and bolted for his life. He journeyed deep into Judah's wilderness, running and running until all his energy faded. Drained and disheartened, Elijah pleaded with God to end his life. End his life? Yes, end his life. The onset of spiritual depression lurks, especially after times of spiritual triumph.

But before we judge Elijah too harshly, we must consider our battles with fear, discouragement, and depression.

Can you remember the last time you felt like running away from your battles, just like Elijah? I've been there, too. One moment you're at the peak of success, and the next, it feels like everything is falling apart. Like when you snagged that promotion on Monday, but by Friday, all your confidence was shattered because self-doubt crept in, leaving you wondering if you could even do the job. Or you graduate from college so excited for what the future holds, but by the time six months pass with no job in sight, anxiety steps in, making you wonder why you ever went to college in the first place. So, how do you stay grounded and keep moving forward?

Occasionally, we all experience discouragement or depression, just like Elijah.

But God knows exactly what we need.

For Elijah, God started with food and rest. An angel fed Elijah and allowed him to get some rest. (1 Kings 19:5-8). After he rested, Elijah had enough strength to walk 40 days to Horeb, the mountain of God. Horeb, also known as Mount Sinai, was where Moses encountered God in the burning bush (Exodus 3:1-2). Next, God spoke to Elijah in a cave at Horeb. This is important because, besides the food and rest, it turns out that Elijah needed time in God's presence. No matter what we're going through, we can all use time in God's presence.

God asked Elijah, "What are you doing here?" Elijah told God how Israel was still in rebellion, that his prophets were dead, and now his life was on the line. After listening to Elijah, God told him to stand at attention on the mountain, and He would pass by. While standing outside the cave, God gave Elijah supernatural illumination (1 Kings 19: 11-14) before asking him again, "What are you doing here?" Elijah gave God the same excuse he had given earlier: "We may have won the battle at Mount Carmel, but it's obvious we lost the war because they destroyed your altars, killed your prophets, and now they are trying to kill me." But what Elijah was missing was that God's power had not diminished. God displayed His power to show Elijah He was still in control.

- So, for every employee who unexpectedly got laid off, God is in control.

- For the couple who wants a baby but can't seem to conceive, God is in control.

- For every mother who lost a child, God is in control.

- For every college student who can't find enough money to pay tuition, God is in control.

- For every woman who hears the words, "You have cancer," God is in control.

God wants us to remember that He is still in control no matter how bad life seems.

TIME TO MAKE ADJUSTMENTS

It didn't take long for me to start feeling discouraged after my cancer diagnosis. Like Elijah, I only wanted to run away and sleep for hours. I kept hoping that when I woke up, I would be cancer free. But I wasn't.

By the time Sunday came, I was emotionally drained. But I wasn't about to hide out in a cave. I wasn't about to give the devil the satisfaction of isolating me from fellowshipping with other believers. I knew that I was in for an uphill battle. But I also knew that I couldn't do it on my own. So, I went to church to hear a message from the Lord. The senior pastor of my church, Dr. T.L. Carmichael, Sr. delivered a sermon titled "*Making Adjustments.*"

As part of that message, I heard God say, "You are the perfect person to go through this trial because you *know* me."

So why not me? I had to ask myself, 'Who better to go through this storm, but me?' Not because I know so much about cancer, but because I KNOW GOD.

And the Spirit of the Lord reminded me that God hadn't left me in the past and won't leave me now.

By the end of the sermon, I had a completely different perspective. Not only had I been chosen to go through this storm, but I had a chance to be like the man in Mark 2:3-5, whose friends tore the roof off the house to lower him down to where Jesus was. As the word says, "When Jesus saw their faith," ...I wanted Jesus to see my faith.

I wanted Jesus to see that I would trust Him, no matter what. I decided to use my faith and walk in victory before the battle was over.

On the morning I heard the sermon, "Making Adjustments," I went to my church saying, "I don't want cancer." But I left saying, 'By the time I'm done walking this thing out, cancer won't want me, either.'

Dear Lord,

You are my light and salvation, so I don't have to fear anything. And because you are my stronghold, I know I don't have to be afraid. With you, God, by my side, I know I can face any obstacle with courage, knowing You will always be there for me. So, whatever I face today, I remember that God is with me every step of the way.

*May your peace and strength fill my heart today and
every day.*

In Jesus' name, Amen.

THE BATTLE IS NOT YOURS OR MINE
Ask God to lead the charge

We must let God lead the way when dealing with a battle or trial. We
must ensure that whatever strategy or plan we choose has been autho-
rized by Him first. When our focus is on following His instructions,
no matter how hard they may be, He will always provide guidance and
assurance throughout each step of the process.

Trust in the Lord to fight your battles

We all face different challenges and difficulties that can be overwhelming, so it's easy to become discouraged. But God does not want
us to run away from our battles—He wants us to trust Him to fight
for us.

Live in peace

Once you have placed your trust in God and allowed Him to lead
you through your battle, live in peace. Knowing that He has already
gone ahead of you and provided a way out will help keep your mind
at ease. No longer running scared of your enemies gives an incredible
sense of relief because now you know beyond a doubt that no matter
what comes your way, He will give you peace.

The spirit of heaviness weighing down my thoughts lifted once I got
a new perspective. I was ready to make a battle plan.

Chapter Three

Get Battle Ready

They will fight against you,
but they shall not prevail
against you, for I am with
you, declares the Lord, to
deliver you.
–Jeremiah 1:19 (ESV)

As a child, I wasn't afraid to fight. As one of a handful of black kids attending a predominantly white elementary school in Campbell, Ohio, I had to be ready for the bullies who wanted to test the girl who was different. I was also shy, so I didn't intentionally look for fights. But anytime a boy chose to cross the imaginary line in the sand on the playground, I was prepared to teach him a lesson. The boys I fought liked pushing girls around. I didn't like being pushed around.

So, when Billy (not his real name) and his friends told me and my friends that we had to move from where we were playing, I was the first to tell him no. Every day during recess, my friends and I played on the edge of the playground. We weren't in the way. We weren't bothering anyone. As a matter of fact, we were minding our own business. Yet, here stood Billy the Bully declaring that he wanted to play in the same spot where my friends and I were standing. Not the spot next to us which we suggested. Not only did we say no, but I had enough fight in me that day to take on Billy.

My cancer diagnosis felt like Billy the Bully; it wanted to take over. But realizing that I was fighting against the spiritual powers of evil in the heavenly places, I wasn't about to let the devil get the best of me. I still don't like to be pushed around by bullies.

I knew immediately that the enemy wanted me to think cancer would take over my life and ultimately defeat me. All he had to do was get me distracted from God. The same God who shows me grace on top of grace. The same God who answered my prayers during previous battles. The exact same God who brought me out of a life of darkness into the light through His Son, Jesus Christ. If the enemy could get me to forget about *that* God, the only wise God our Savior, then he knew he would beat me in the battle.

I wasn't about to give him what he wanted. So, I went to God's word for comfort and meditated on Jeremiah 1:19.

> "They will fight against you, but they shall not prevail against you, for I am with you, declares the Lord, to deliver you."

Instead of fearing what this disease could do to me, I embraced it as an opportunity to stand on God's promise to fight for me. But I also knew it was important to humble myself and follow God's plan. So, I offered God this prayer.

Dear Jesus,

I sincerely thank you for your mighty presence and support, which has guided me through every challenge. Your grace has given me the strength and freedom to overcome emotional, spiritual, and mental struggles. I humbly ask for your forgiveness for allowing myself to remain trapped longer than necessary by failing to embrace the truth within your word. Jesus, I pray that your name, the Mighty God, resounds within me so profoundly that it silences the deceitful whispers of the enemy. In all humility, I seek your forgiveness.

In the name of Jesus, I pray. Amen.

Instead of being intimidated by cancer, I decided to confront it head-on. In my prayer time with God, I first asked for His will to be done. I thought this was important because I didn't want to come off as bossing God around. Instead, I said, "If it is your will, Lord, I would like to:

- Continue taking care of my family.

- Attend church and fellowship with other believers.

- Be healthy enough to work every day.

- Make a conscious effort to be kind to everyone, especially the doctors, nurses, and staff you have assigned to take care of me.

- Not be overcome by the medicines needed to treat my disease.

- Be grateful every day.

Next, I purchased a special cancer care journal for recording all my doctor's appointments, notes about my treatment options, and progress. Once I scheduled all my doctor visits and medical appointments, I bought a few items to get me through chemotherapy treatments like:

- An electric blanket

- Chemo shirt, gloves, and socks

- A neck pillow

- Oncology cream for radiation

My first chemotherapy session was set for Monday, November 22, 2021, three days before Thanksgiving. Remembering my grandmother's instructions on my first day of kindergarten, I walked into the UNC Rex Cancer Center with my head held high and ready to fight.

THERE HAS TO BE A BETTER WAY

How do you get ready for battle? Sometimes you can see a battle on the horizon. Other times, your battle pops up out of nowhere. No one can escape life's battles. But the problem with battles is that they are unpredictable. You don't always know when you'll be in the fight of your life. In light of this truth, knowing how to stay ready for a battle is hard.

Now, the devil is always ready. God's Word is clear that he is a thief that comes to kill, steal and destroy (John 10:10). So, we all know that the enemy will use anything to his advantage to defeat you in battle. But what about you? What steps do you take to become battle ready? In 1 Peter 5:6-11, we find Peter's instructions to the church in anticipation of a "fiery trial." His advice applies to you and me and any trial we might encounter.

Humble yourselves, therefore, under the mighty hand of God so that at the proper time, he may exalt you, casting all your anxieties on him because he cares for you. Be sober-minded; be watchful. Your adversary the devil, prowls around like a roaring lion, seeking someone to devour. Resist him, firm in your faith, knowing that the same kinds of suffering are being experienced by your brotherhood throughout the world. And after you have suffered a little while, the God of all grace, who has called you to his eternal glory in Christ, will himself restore, confirm, strengthen, and establish you. To him be the dominion forever and ever. Amen.

Be humble

It's easy to want to elevate yourself based on your title, name, or position. In the midst of your battle, you might be tempted to say, "Do these people know who I am? I'm an important person, and I expect to be recognized as such." God does not like the sin of pride. After all, it was pride that caused Lucifer to turn into Satan. Instead, God asks that we humble ourselves so He can promote us at the right time.

Be watchful

God's Word is clear that Satan is a thief that comes to kill, steal and destroy (John 10:10). Because he is a formidable enemy with many demons, we shouldn't ignore him, joke about him, or underestimate his determination to destroy us. We must "be sober" and stay connected to God.

Be mindful

We are not the only people being attacked by Satan. Peter reminds us that our brothers and sisters worldwide have the same sufferings that we have. Being mindful of the struggles that others face around the world is an important aspect of living a compassionate and empathetic life. As humans, it can be easy to become absorbed in our own problems and forget that others may share similar sufferings. By staying mindful of the fact that we are part of a larger community, we can learn to be more understanding, supportive, and kind toward others.

LESSONS FROM SCRIPTURE: Naaman Has a Change of Heart

Naaman was angry. His trip to Samaria wasn't going how he thought it would. First, he went to see King Joram with a letter from the king of Aram that conveyed the message: "Cure my military commander." (2 Kings 5:4-6) Unfortunately, Israel's King Joram didn't have a relationship with God, let alone faith that Naaman would find the healing he needed. Instead, Joram saw Naaman's visit as a cleverly disguised attempt by the king of Aram to start a fight. Flustered and afraid, King Joram had a panic attack. When Elisha found out the king was in distress, he asked him to send Naaman to him so that "he would know there was a prophet in Israel."

So, Naaman goes to see Elisha. Upon arriving at Elisha's house, he was left standing at the door. Not only did Elisha not answer the door, he didn't even say hello to Naaman. There was no red carpet. There was no marching band. No ticker-tape parade to celebrate his arrival. Instead, Naaman got a message from Elisha through one of his servants, "Wash seven times in the Jordan River to be healed." (2 Kings 5:10)

Can you hear God say to Naaman, "Yes, Naaman, if you want to be healed, this is part of the process?" It's easy to imagine what God is saying to others around us. But can you hear what God is saying to you about your healing? This was a question I had to ask myself. But let's get back to Naaman.

"I thought he'd personally come out and meet me, call on the name of God, wave his hand over the diseased spot, and get rid of the disease. The Damascus rivers, Abana and Pharpar, are cleaner than any of the rivers in Israel." And with that, Naaman stomped off. (2 Kings 5:11-12) Because of pride, Naaman got mad and left.

It was clear to see that Naaman was a proud and conceited man. He was a great captain of the army of the king of Aram. Naaman was a great and powerful man who knew it by all accounts. He was important. The Lord used Naaman to lead Aram to victory. But what Naaman didn't realize was that his victories weren't because of his doing. Every victory Naaman won was a gift from God.

So one of his servants tried to reason with him, "Father, if the prophet has asked you to do something hard and heroic, wouldn't you have done it, so why not this simple, 'wash and be clean'?" (2 Kings 5:13). In other words, will you pass up the chance to be healed just because the cure was as simple as putting your body into the water?

So, he did it. Naaman gave in and dipped himself in the Jordan seven times. Just like that, Naaman's skin was restored. He was healed.

For a few minutes, it looked like Naaman would miss out on his blessing. Has this ever happened to you? Oh, sure, it has. You need healing, deliverance, or some other breakthrough, and the devil tries to distract you. The enemy whispers in your ear to tell you that you are special. Your name is great. Your job is great. Your position in society is great. Because you are so great, God should recognize your greatness. After all, you're YOU.

If we're not careful, the devil will talk us right out of our healing, deliverance, or breakthrough.

What started out as me saying, 'Oh, no, I hope I don't have cancer,' could have easily turned into, "Why do *I* have to have cancer? I've accomplished a lot in my life and career. I made my way from *that* side of town to *this* side of town. I've paid my dues. I was the ten-year-old girl whose grandfather died on Sunday morning and after spending all of Monday morning making funeral arrangements with my mother, came home to find out my father died on Monday afternoon. Haven't I been through enough in this life? Haven't I cried enough tears?"

The devil wanted me to go there, and he wants you to go there too. But we must turn around and say, "Anyway, you bless me, Lord, I'll be satisfied."

When we look back at Naaman, did he really have a problem with the way Elisha delivered the message from the Lord to him? Did he really have a problem with the idea of going into the Jordan River? On the surface, it looked like Naaman had a problem with those things, but his real problem was what was happening inside himself. Naaman went to Samaria, thinking he would receive a quick fix for his problem. But God didn't just want to heal Naaman's body. God wanted to heal Naaman's heart. When Elisha told the king of Israel that this visitor would soon know there was a prophet in the land, it was not for his glory but for God's glory. Not only did Naaman learn to humble himself, but he also learned that the God of Israel was the one true God.

Naaman came with enough money to buy his healing. But when he tried to leave an offering, Elisha refused to take it because his services were not for sale. Do you know what's interesting? Despite the money Naaman's king gave him to buy his healing, he actually left Samaria indebted to God. No matter how hard we try, we can't beat God's giving.

When we're sick, distressed, or faced with life's latest battle, we must humble ourselves before the Lord. Don't let the devil trick you into thinking you can walk up to God and snatch your blessing from his hands. No. Listen to the voice of God. Follow the instructions from the Lord. Be willing to change. Let go of all pretenses. It is He who has made us and not we ourselves (Psalm 100:3). God doesn't owe us anything, but He wants to give us everything according to His will for our lives.

God will use life's battles to change us from the inside out.

NEW OUTLOOK
Go to God in humble submission
Naaman's unbelief in Elisha's instructions almost cost him his healing. But when he humbled himself and followed Elisha's directions, he was finally cured. His pride and position blinded him so much that he couldn't see the truth right before him. It was only through the help of others and his own willingness to listen that he finally understood.
Don't tell God how to handle His business
Naaman was insulted that Elisha didn't come out to speak to him, and he was skeptical that washing in the Jordan River would cure him.

Naaman's servant begged him to do as Elisha commanded, and finally, Naaman did. To his amazement, he was cured of his leprosy. However, it's important to note that he had to be humbled first. Naaman was a proud and powerful man, but he had to humble himself to receive his healing.

Recognize the power of God

Towards the end of the story, Naaman confessed that the God of Israel was the one true God. This confession shows that Naaman didn't just experience physical healing but spiritual healing as well. He realized there was something more significant than his power and position in life. He acknowledged that God, the one true God, was in control.

MAKE A BATTLE PLAN

Are you ready to make a battle plan? I can tell you that after I:

- Heard God's voice about making adjustments,

- Prayed and meditated on God's word,

- Identified the things I wanted to do, but only if they aligned with God's plan, and

- Organized my calendar

I was ready to create a battle plan. I had a new resolve and a new perspective. I knew that to be victorious in Christ, I would have to align my actions with God's plan. So I created a battle strategy called: I won't, but I will.

1. I won't fight in fear, but I will suit up for battle.

2. I won't panic, but I will be prepared to pray.

3. I won't let the enemy control my mind, but I will renew my

mind.

4. I won't cower in the corner, but I will stand tall with other believers.

5. I won't wave a white flag, but I will walk in victory.

I've been in lots of fights. But for this one, I knew I had to fight more strategically than I had before. No more running. I knew I needed a renewed heart and mind.

Chapter Four

Strategy #1 – I Will Suit Up for Battle

Put on all of God's armor so that you will be able to stand safe against all strategies and tricks of Satan.

-Ephesians 6:11 TLB

T he air was thick with smoke, and the crackle of burning wood filled the ears of the brave firefighters who had come to battle the raging wildfire. The firefighters were equipped with all of the necessary personal protective equipment – fire-resistant pants and shirts, helmets, eye protection, gloves, leather boots, and a fire shelter – but they also had their personal gear bags packed with plenty of water and rations in case they needed it. In addition to these items, each firefighter carried two hand tools: a Pulaski and McLeod.

The Pulaski was used primarily for digging up soil or chopping wood as required. At the same time, its counterpart, the McLeod, featured both tooth-like blades on one side for raking fire lines plus a large hoe-like blade at its other end, which could be utilized when tackling fires from different angles. With these tools, nothing stood between them and success - just hard work ahead.

And so it went – hour after hour as these heroic firefighters worked tirelessly towards extinguishing these stubborn flames. Finally, after several long hours – their efforts paid off as cheers rang through the air celebrating victory over an enemy that had threatened so many lives before its demise.

If you and I want to put out the battles in our lives that come at us like raging forest fires, we need to have the kind of equipment Paul talks about in Ephesians 6.

> *Put on all of God's ar-*
> *mor so that you will be able*
> *to stand safe against all*
> *strategies and tricks of Sa-*
> *tan.*
> *Ephesians 6:11*

PUT ON THE WHOLE ARMOR

We can't go into battle without the tools we need to win. Since we've established that our battle is spiritual, then we must wear the armor God has given us to stand against the enemy. As the apostle Paul said, "Be strong in the Lord and in His mighty power. Put on all of

God's armor so that you can stand firm against the devil's schemes."
(Ephesians 6:10-11).

To understand how to put on the armor of God, let's first identify
what the armor actually is. In his teachings, Paul uses Roman soldiers
as a model for us to recognize and combat the forces of evil. The Roman soldiers were renowned for their power and strength during this
time. Paul draws parallels between the armor they wore and what God
has given us in the spiritual realm. Let's examine Ephesians 6:14-17.

- Stand firm then, with the *belt of truth buckled around your
  waist*,

- with the *breastplate of righteousness* in place,

- and with your *feet fitted with the readiness that comes from
  the gospel of peace.*

- In addition to all this, *take up the shield of faith*, with which
  you can extinguish all the flaming arrows of the evil one.

- Take the *helmet of salvation*

- and the *sword of the Spirit*, which is the word of God. (Ephesians 6:14-17)

Stand firm then, with the *belt of truth buckled around your waist*

When Roman soldiers went to war, they would tuck their clothing
into their belts to secure it tightly for easy movement during battle.
To "stand firm" means standing in front of and opposing the forces
and plans of evil. *Truth* is the standard by which reality is measured.
God's Word is truth. Wearing "truth like a belt" means living genuinely

before God. Starting with truth prepares you for battle since the devil is a liar and cannot operate in an environment of integrity.

The *breastplate of righteousness*

To stand strong against the enemy's attacks, we must wear righteousness like a shield to protect our hearts. God has given us Christ's perfect righteousness. So, when the devil tries to accuse us, we can confidently stand in the truth of our righteous position in Christ. But it's not just about knowing the truth, but also living it out daily. When we choose to live righteously, we close the door to the enemy and prevent him from gaining a foothold in our hearts and lives.

Feet fitted with the readiness that comes from the gospel of peace

Roman soldiers wore sandals with built-in cleats to provide stability to stand their ground during attacks. In Ephesians, it emphasizes the importance of standing firm repeatedly. The enemy can easily undermine our stability by tempting us with worry. When we carry anxiety and worry, we lose our peace. However, when we live righteously, we can experience God's peace, which confirms that we align with His will.

Take up the shield of faith

When Paul wrote this passage, Roman soldiers used large shields made from wood and covered with thick animal hide. These shields were shaped to allow soldiers to interlock them, creating a strong line of defense against enemies. As the enemy's arrows were often dipped in a flammable substance and set on fire, the soldiers would quickly dip their shields into the water to extinguish the flames and protect themselves.

Similarly, faith serves as a powerful defensive weapon that safeguards our hearts and minds from the attacks of Satan. Just as the Roman soldiers regularly immersed their shields in water to keep them strong and effective, our faith must be continually nourished and fortified by immersing ourselves in God's word. Our faith grows by hearing and studying God's word, enabling us to stand strong against our challenges. And as we journey through life, it is important for us to unite our faith with other believers, standing together in times of battle.

Take the *helmet of salvation*

The helmet of salvation, comparable to the breastplate of right-eousness, relies not only on Christ's redemptive work but also on our cooperation as we walk alongside the Lord. In Isaiah 59:17, God is the divine warrior who puts on the helmet of salvation.

Satan seeks to attack our minds, but the helmet metaphor rep-resents the mind controlled by God. It is crucial to safeguard our thoughts by maintaining a strong spiritual standing in Christ. This involves allowing Him to permeate every aspect of our thinking. Keep in mind that the primary battleground for spiritual warfare is our minds. While the enemy aims to bind us with strongholds, the Lord imparts liberating truth to reshape our mindsets.

The *sword of the Spirit*

The sword is a vital part of the armor, serving both defensive and offensive purposes. Paul uses a term that does not refer to a long sword but to a dagger used in close combat. He refers to the Word of God, spoken and made powerful by the Spirit to expose and overcome Satan's deceitful lies. As believers, when faced with temptation, our most powerful weapon is God's Word.

In verse 18, Paul ends with prayer, the heavenly way of equipping ourselves with spiritual armor. This practice reflects the life and sacri-fice of Jesus Christ, which benefits us greatly. As Christians, we access our spiritual resources through open and personal communication with God. For this reason, we must always be ready to pray. To access heaven's authority for intervention on earth, it is important to communicate regularly with God and pray in the Spirit. Aligning ourselves with the Spirit and utilizing spiritual wisdom is key. One of the most effective methods is to pray God's Word back to him and apply it to our life.

LESSONS FROM SCRIPTURE: Jesus is Tempted

Jesus had been fasting and praying for forty days and nights, and even during this time of spiritual meditation, he was not exempt from temptation. Suddenly, Satan appeared before him with an offer to give him all the kingdoms of the world if only he bowed down to worship him. But Jesus remained resolute in his faith. Each time Satan tried to sway Him away from His Father's will, Jesus replied with three simple but powerful words - "It is written."

Satan knew these words well since they were part of God's Word. It became clear that although Satan could quote Scripture selectively to confuse and misguide people, Jesus knew it intimately to be able to defend against any deceptions thrown at Him, with each successive temptation rebuffed by this holy weapon – The Word of God – Satan eventually gave up and slinked into the shadows.

This is why we must take our cues from Christ by being deeply acquainted with every word given to us by God through His Holy Scriptures so that when faced with any form of temptation or deception, we can stand firm on what has been written rather than letting ourselves be swayed away from His truth.

Before leaving the house, make sure you have on God's armor. Before you board a flight for your next business trip, don't forget God's armor. Before you get in line at the unemployment office, make sure you're wearing God's armor. Before you run out the door to go to your doctor's appointment, don't leave home without God's armor.

In other words, if you follow Jesus Christ, you must wear God's armor. Your outer garments can come from any brand you want – Ralph Lauren, Banana Republic, Target, Walmart, the Salvation Army, the flea market – but your spiritual attire must be God's armor.

Why? Because wearing God's armor is the only way you will be able to stand against the devil's schemes. Wear the pristine and powerful Armor of God to triumph over the devil's cunning plans. Remember, our enemy is not people, but the dark rulers, authorities, and spiritual powers lurking in the heavenly realm. With God's complete armor, you will be unbeatable against worldly darkness and stand strong on the day of evil. Once the fight is finished, you will still stand tall, steadfast in your faith.

The journey through cancer can be hard. Once diagnosed with stage 2 breast cancer, I met with doctors and nurses to discuss my treatment plan. Beginning in November 2021, I had to have eight cycles of chemotherapy, a lumpectomy, and 30 radiation sessions. Because I was invited to participate in a study to determine if less chemotherapy is needed to treat patients, my number of chemotherapy treatments was reduced to six cycles. In addition, I made several trips to the doctor for MRIs, echocardiograms, mammograms, port placement, and more. Through all of this, I wore God's armor.

Ephesians 6:10-20 is powerful because it represents a call to battle in a spiritual war. The style and form of the letter have been compared to a "peroration," or a peroratio, where an author or general summarizes the main theme of a letter or speech to motivate an audience to take action. Verses 10-13 offer an invitation to be empowered by God's power. The battle imagery is brought to life in verses 14-17 through the image of a warrior outfitted with God's armor as clad in truth, justice, faith, and salvation, ready to announce peace and wield God's word. The metaphoric battle ends in verses 18-20, focusing on prayer and solidarity among Christians in war.

The warrior in this Scripture is you. It's me.

It's important to recognize that Satan will try to prevent you from putting on God's armor and focusing on the spiritual realm. He knows that by diverting your attention elsewhere, he can keep you from finding the victory you are looking for. It's his mission to distract you with the things you can experience through your feelings. Don't let him! Stay focused on God and the resources He offers to help you win every battle.

YOU HAVE EVERYTHING YOU NEED TO WIN

Stay ready

The enemy can attack at any time, which is why you have to stay battle-ready. Going into battle unarmed is a big no-no. Since our battle is spiritual, we must put on the armor provided by God to resist the devil. That's why we must gear up with God's armor to face the enemy head-on. Like Paul said, "Get strong in the Lord and flex His mighty power. Suit up with God's armor and show the devil who's boss" (Ephesians 6:10-11).

Keep your sword sharp

If you want to defend yourself against the enemy, you better keep your sword sharp. Just like Jesus, who used the Word of God to thwart the devil's schemes, we need to ensure that we are well-versed in Scripture to face whatever challenges come our way. Don't be caught off guard or unprepared in the face of temptation or trials. Keep your sword sharp through daily Bible study, prayer, and fellowship with other believers. With the right attitude and weapon, you can overcome anything Satan throws at you.

You are more than a conqueror

One of Satan's tactics is to make us feel inadequate or weak. He tries to make us think we are not enough and will never measure up. But God's word tells us that we are fearfully and wonderfully made. We are children of God and have everything we need to conquer whatever comes our way. When we are filled with God's extraordinary power, we can overcome any obstacle. We can be confident that we can stand against the darkness, knowing we have victory through Christ.

Chapter Five

Strategy #2 – I Will Be Prepared To Pray

> *Do not be anxious about anything, but in every situation, by prayer and petition, with thanksgiving, present your requests to God.*
> -Philippians 4:6 NIV

George Müller, a missionary serving in Bristol, England, during the early 1800s, left an indelible legacy through the schools and orphanages he established. His humble account of God's miraculous assistance in providing necessities for countless destitute children he looked after continues to inspire our faith even today.

As night descended over the harbor of Bristol, England, the children of the Müller orphanage were getting ready for bed. Amidst this peaceful routine, a sudden crisis struck - they had run out of milk for the morning oatmeal. Just then, George Müller was working in his study when his wife arrived with the alarming news. What would the orphans have for breakfast tomorrow?

George paused and carefully set aside his pen. It wasn't the first time the funds for food and other supplies ran low. The Müllers had taken in their first group of thirty girls in 1836, and now, their orphanage was overflowing with more than a hundred faces in need. From the beginning, George made a solemn promise to himself: he would never ask for funds from anyone, nor would he borrow money. For George, there was only one avenue, one source of help he could rely on - God. Through his complete trust in the Lord's faithfulness, George saw His abundant provisions repeatedly.

As Mueller rose from his desk, he grabbed his wife's hand and invited two employees to join him in prayer. "Mary," he said calmly, "let us pray." The door creaked open, and two employees from the orphanage walked in, taking their place alongside Mueller and his wife. Together, they made their humble request to God, knowing that tiny, helpless mouths depended on them for their next meal. As the prayer ended, George reminded them, "Be assured, if you walk with Him and look to Him and expect help from Him, He will never fail you."

Suddenly, there was a knock at the door. After answering the door, Mary returned to the study with an envelope. "George, you have to see this!" she exclaimed. Inside the envelope was more than enough money for the milk. Before they could catch their breath, two more letters arrived with generous pledges of support.

George Müller's unwavering faith in God's Word was a game-changer. It was common for Müller to experience an immediate and bountiful response to prayer. As a pastor, he lived without a salary, trusting only in the kindness of those who believed in his mission. Once he discovered faith and committed himself to studying the Scriptures, he trusted God's Word.

George and his wife took Paul at his word when he said:

> *Do not be anxious about anything, but in every situation, by prayer and petition, with thanksgiving, present your requests to God.* (Phil 4:6)

George reminds me of my grandmother, Lucille Singletary. When times got tough, she didn't cower; she prayed. My grandmother's prayers were intentional, specific, deliberate, and strategic. Yes, she prayed without ceasing. My grandmother made prayer a faithful practice, pouring her heart into every word. She was grateful every time prayers were answered with immediate and abundant blessings. Grandma even asked her Heavenly Father to stir the hearts of those around her, which is part of why I am here today. I had a praying grandmother.

I also had a praying mother and brother, along with praying aunts, uncles, real cousins, 'play' cousins, and friends. To top everything off, God even blessed me with a praying husband and a beautiful church family led by a dynamic pastor and his wife, who offered me a proper education on prayer. I have been in the presence of some of the mightiest prayer warriors ever to live.

So why did it take me so long to learn that prayer should be my first option, not my last? Why did I waste so much time trying to fix the problem alone or fight the enemy by myself? Because despite the relationship I had with people who pray, I had to develop a prayer life for myself. And in doing so, I had to learn one of the most important lessons of my life: Not only is prayer an act of communication with God, but prayer is a weapon. I had to learn to use prayer to knock out the enemy. And once I learned how to use prayer as a weapon, things changed. I changed.

> *Dear God,*
>
> *I humbly come before you in the name of Jesus, acknowledging you as El Roi, the God who sees me. Because you see me, I know you know the battle I am currently facing. Just as you saw Abraham's trust in you and provided a ram as Jehovah Jireh, I believe you see me and will provide for my needs. Please forgive me for failing to see the one who sees me. Thank you for your attentiveness and for listening to my prayers. Please see the diligence of my heart and open doors that only you can open. I ask for your favor to be upon me.*
> *In Jesus' name, Amen.*

What do you bet Satan never wanted me to learn this lesson about prayer? He doesn't want you to learn about the power of prayer, either. Why? Because when you use prayer to stay connected to God, a few important things happen.

- God draws close to us when we call Him (Psalm 145:18)

- We don't have to worry (Phil 4:6)

- God hears our prayers (1 John 5:14)

- God will tell us things (Jeremiah 33:3)

- Sins confessed are sins forgiven (1 John 1:9)

This list could go on. But the bottom line is this - you can use prayer for every battle in your life. Don't let the enemy distract you from using this powerful tool. When worry sets in, pray. When fear knocks on the door of your heart, pray. When debt tries to overtake your life, pray. When sickness tries to weigh you down, pray.

Stop letting the enemy push you around, play with your mind, and upset your spirit. Go to God in prayer every time. When we take our cares and concerns to the Lord, there's a promise in Philippians 4:7, "And the peace of God, which transcends all understanding, will guard your hearts and your minds in Christ Jesus."

LESSONS FROM SCRIPTURE: King Jehoshaphat Takes His Fears to the Father

Do you know who used prayer before a battle? King Jehoshaphat. There was a battle brewing on the horizon of King Jehoshaphat's life. The Moabites, Ammonites, and Meunites had their sights set on taking out Jehoshaphat. They united their forces in an attempt to overthrow him. When Jehoshaphat received this information, he was afraid. It was clear that a massive opposing force was en route and already at the oasis of Engedi.

But Jehoshaphat didn't lose heart. He didn't run around panicked. He didn't call ten friends to talk about how unfair life was. He didn't get drunk. He didn't run scared. Instead, he prayed to God for help. Not only did he pray, but he called for a fast across the land. People from every nook and cranny of Judah answered the call, gathering in unison to seek divine intervention.

What do you do when you know a battle is headed your way?

Next, Jehoshaphat stood before the people of Judah and Jerusalem at The Temple of God, a grand structure that radiated majesty. You can almost hear his voice ringing passionately,

> *"O God, God of our ancestors, you are the mighty ruler of all kingdoms below and above. Your power is unparalleled and unmatched - no one can stand up against you! When you drove out the natives of this land and gave it to your people Israel, they built this holy house of worship to worship you. In times of war, floods, disease, or famine, our people raised their voices in prayer here, knowing that you were personally present in this place and would listen to their cries for help.*

> *But now, dear God, men from Ammon, Moab, and Mount Seir threaten us. Even though we bypassed them earlier when we arrived here, they've come to drive us away from our land! O our Lord, please come to our rescue! We're at their mercy and don't know what to do. We're looking up to you for salvation."* (2 Chronicles 20:6-12)

Jehoshaphat's prayer was clear and specific. Knowing that we can pray when we need God to help us is a joy.

Everyone who lived in Judah was there - little children, wives, sons- all present and eager to hear from God. Suddenly, Jahaziel was moved by the Spirit of God to address the congregation. If you don't know, Jahaziel was a Levite from the Asaph clan – his father was Zechariah, his grandfather Benaiah, his great-grandfather Jeiel and his great-great-grandfather Mattaniah. His name meant *seeing God*. So, Jahaziel stepped forward to say, "Attention everyone--whether you're from out of town, from Jerusalem, or King Jehoshaphat – listen closely to God's word. Don't be afraid or pay attention to this wave of vandals. This is God's battle, not yours."

Every battle that comes in your life, you are to give it to God. He will tell you what He wants you to do in every situation. And, because every battle is different, His instructions will be tailor-made for you and your battle. Remember, we are not fighting against people made of flesh and blood, but against persons without bodies—the evil rulers of the unseen world, those mighty satanic beings and great evil princes of darkness who rule this world, and against huge numbers of wicked spirits in the spirit world. (Ephesians 6:12)

So, the battle with your boss belongs to God. The battle with your next-door neighbor belongs to God. Your battle with cancer belongs to God.

Jahaziel told everyone, "Tomorrow you will march towards them; they're already heading up the slopes of Ziz. You will meet them at the end of the ravine near the wilderness of Jeruel. But you won't even have to lift a finger during this battle. All you have to do is stand firm, Judah and Jerusalem, and witness God's saving work unfold before your very eyes. Do not be afraid, and do not waver. Boldly march out tomorrow and remember, God is with you."

With this powerful declaration, Jehoshaphat and his people of Judah and Jerusalem knelt before God, worshiping with their faces to the ground. The Kohathite and Korahite Levites stood up, singing praises at the top of their lungs. At dawn, they marched towards Tekoa's wilderness with zeal.

Jehoshaphat encouraged the people, "Believe in your God! Have faith in your prophets and you will be victorious!" After discussing a plan, he led a robe-clad choir singing praises to God:

"Thanks to God above!

His steadfast love!"

With the choir's shout and the start of praise, God set ambushes against the men of Ammon, Moab, and Mount Seir, as they were attacking Judah. The Ammonites and Moabites were disoriented and mistakenly killed many from Mount Seir. Next, utterly confused, they attacked each other and ultimately met their downfall.

As Judah peered over the hilltop, gazing upon a deserted battlefield littered with corpses, they knew they won against the horde of barbarians. When Jehoshaphat and his people approached, intending to collect the spoils, they found treasures more bountiful than they could carry. It took three whole days to transport the immeasurable wealth, including everything from equipment and clothing to valuable trinkets. Finally, on the fourth day, they reached the Valley of Blessing (Beracah), where they honored and praised God for the blessings He bestowed upon His people.

As their band instruments rang throughout the valley, Jehoshaphat led his people in an exuberant parade, rejoicing in the joyful relief God had gifted them. Their procession concluded when they reached The Temple of God, giving thanks and praise to the Almighty.

Upon hearing how God had championed Israel's enemies, the surrounding kingdoms trembled in fear of divine retribution, and Jehoshaphat was met with unbridled peace throughout his reign as king.

FEAR NOT

Take your fears to the Father

It is natural to feel fear in life, whether it be in regard to our health, relationships, or future plans. However, as believers, we are not called to let our fears consume us. Instead, we are called to take our fears to the Father. Much like Jehoshaphat, who turned to God in prayer before a battle, we, too, can find comfort and strength through prayer and trusting in the Lord. As we take our fears to Him, we can be reminded of His love, His sovereignty, and His promises for our lives. Our victory may not always come in the form we expect, but we can have faith that the Lord will work all things together for our good.

Go to God first

When faced with a problem or difficult situation, it's easy to turn to human solutions first. However, Jehoshaphat's example reminds us that we should go to God as our first response. As we learn from Jehoshaphat's story, he didn't hesitate to call upon the Lord, seeking His guidance and Divine intervention. God is all-knowing and all-powerful and can provide us with the wisdom and strength we need to overcome any obstacle we may face.

Trust and believe that God's power is greater than our problems

Life can throw us some unexpected curveballs, but it's important to remember that God's power is greater than any problem we have or will face. It's easy to get caught up in the overwhelming feeling of life's problems and feel like there's no way out, but when we shift our focus from the problem to what only God can do, things start to look a lot different.

When you start believing that God's power is greater than any problem you face, your life will start changing for the better. You'll become more confident when facing difficult decisions because He will always come through for you, no matter what. You'll also feel calmer and more secure knowing that the Lord is always by your side, ready to help guide you down the path of righteousness—even if it doesn't lead directly to where you want to go! And finally, you'll be able to make peace with whatever outcome awaits because you understand that whatever happens was meant by Him for your highest good.

God Can Help Us Overcome Anything

Sometimes the challenges we face seem impossible to overcome. Whether it's personal struggles, family issues, or global crises, it's easy to feel powerless and alone. However, it's important to remember that God is always with us and always ready to help. With faith and trust in His power, we can overcome anything that comes our way. By laying our burdens at His feet, we can find strength, peace, and hope to keep moving forward. With God by our side, all things are possible, and we can have the courage to face each day with confidence, perseverance, and love.

Chapter Six

Strategy #3 – I Will Renew My Mind

Do not conform to the pattern of this world, but be transformed by the renewing of your mind. Then you will be able to test and approve what God's will is—his good, pleasing, and perfect will.
-Romans 12:2 NIV

Standing on the rocky shore, you look out at the beautiful ocean. You can't believe you're finally here on your first extreme vacation. Watching the final episode of *Survivor* convinced you to take the plunge, so you flew halfway around the world to get to a secluded island in the middle of nowhere. You imagined this day for months. It's everything you thought it would be, except you are completely alone.

You thought you signed up for the group package. You imagined being stranded with other people with the same love for extreme adventures. Working side by side as a team. Someone would build a fire. Someone else would forage for food. Another group of people would set up a tent or build a fort. But that's not happening. It's all on you for the next 15 days.

After saying goodbye to your guide, you take a deep breath and look around the island. You need to figure out where to begin. What do you do first? Do you start a fire to stay warm, look for shelter before it rains, or find food before it gets dark? You start out feeling optimistic, but after a few minutes pass, anxiety creeps in. You begin to question yourself and your abilities. What if you can't do this? What will happen then?

To make matters worse, you don't have any tools with you. No matches. No flashlight. No knife. Nothing. You're starting to doubt you can do this at all.

Does this sound like a vacation you want to take? Me neither. But that doesn't mean we haven't gone through challenging experiences.

We can all relate to how the traveler on the deserted island feels. Out of options. Out of ideas. Out of energy. Out of time. Out of our element. For many people, life feels like being on a deserted island. Instead of standing on the rocky shores, we're standing at the door to divorce court. Instead of looking for fish to cook over an open fire, we're trying to scrape together enough food to feed our children. We don't hear the sounds of wild animals moving around in the bushes, but we do hear doctors and nurses discussing your treatment options. There's debt and bills instead of dirt and bugs. Our predators are our creditors.

And then there are the mind games where you say things like, "Why did I ever think I could do this? I have never been smart enough, or athletic enough, or good enough."

But this is not how your Heavenly Father wants you to think. Now the enemy, this is exactly how he wants you to think. Because he knows that if he can control your mind, then he can control your actions. As part of his master plan to destroy you, he doesn't want you to think you can be successful at anything. Whenever you even think about moving forward or overcoming an obstacle, Satan does his best to flood your mind with doubt, fear, and negative self-talk.

Well, it's time to put an end to Satan's reign over your mind. This is how I took control of my mind.

> *Don't copy the behavior and*
> *customs of this world, but be*
> *a new and different person*
> *with a fresh newness in all*
> *you do and think. Then you*
> *will learn from your own*
> *experience how his ways will*
> *really satisfy you.*
> (Romans 12:2)

True dedication to God involves us giving Him our minds. The message of Paul's letter to the church in Romans Chapter 12 holds true for every believer today: Don't let the world control your mind; let God transform your mind.

In Romans 12:1-2, Paul stresses the importance of taking action in presenting ourselves to God. This is part of building a relationship with God. Paul further explains that by renewing our minds, we can achieve this goal. Paul establishes a cause-and-effect relationship between the renewal of our minds and our transformation. It is crucial to note that verse 2 goes beyond mere guidance; Paul exhorts us to actively pursue this transformation. Our minds are not renewed by God alone. God doesn't just renew our minds without any effort on our part.

Instead, we are called to *personally* renew our minds. So, if you want the renewed mind that Paul talks about in Romans 12:2, you must take action. One way to renew our minds is by obeying God's Word in our pursuit of righteousness. Through daily renewal, we experience a transformation in character, gradually becoming less conformed to the patterns of this world. It's not surprising that holiness requires our continuous effort and commitment.

Are you tired of having your thoughts controlled by the enemy? Renew your mind. Are you tired of being pushed around by Satan? Renew your mind. With a renewed mind that's being transformed by God's word, not only will we walk in the newness of life, but we will start to see ourselves as God sees us. Pray this prayer.

Dear God,

I come to you now, Lord, thanking you for every blessing in my life because I know every good and perfect gift comes from you. Please forgive me, Lord, for the times I let fear, doubt, and shame take over my mind and confuse my thinking. I ask, in the name of Jesus, for a renewed mind. A mind focused on healing, rather than sickness. A mind focused on a debt-free life rather than financial troubles. A mind focused on serving you rather than only serving myself. Change me, Lord, from the inside out.

In Jesus's name, Amen.

LESSONS FROM SCRIPTURE: Gideon

Throughout the Bible, we find God calling people for a purpose. Some were ready to take God at His word and accept their assignment. Others who didn't see themselves as worthy of being called by God needed a little more convincing. One person who comes to mind is Gideon.

One day, an angel of God visited Gideon, who was working hard at threshing wheat in a winepress far away from the meddling Midianites. The angel greeted him with what seemed like a twisted joke: "God is with you, O mighty warrior!" (Judges 6:12)

Gideon's reply was equally bleak. "With me, my master? If God is with us, why has all this happened to us? Where are all the miracle-wonders that our parents told us about, like how God delivered us from Egypt? Honestly, God doesn't care about us. Instead, he has given us up to the Midianites." (v.13)

God told Gideon, "Go in the strength that is yours. Deliver Israel from Midian. Haven't I just sent you?" But Gideon was not convinced. "Me, my master? How could I possibly save Israel? I come from the weakest clan in Manasseh, and I'm the runt of the litter." (v.15)

In response, God offered some reassuring words. "I will be with you. Believe me, you will defeat Midian as one man." Still hesitant, Gideon asked for a sign from God to back up what he was hearing. "If you're serious about this, do me a favor: give me a sign to support what you're telling me. Don't leave until I return and bring you my gift."

Gideon rose with the sun the following morning, accompanied by his entire army. They assembled their camp at Harod Spring while the camp of Midian lay to the north of them, spanning the plain and leading up to the Hill of Moreh.

Divine words were whispered in Gideon's ear, "Your army is too vast for conquest. I will not allow Midian to fall with the hands of so many soldiers that will forget about me upon their victory. Gather your troops and make known this proclamation, 'Anyone afraid or unable to fight may leave Mount Gilead now and go home." 22 companies decided to depart, and only ten remained.

But even still, God spoke. "There are still too many. Take them down to the stream and I'll make the final cuts, those who I say go with you shall join you." Gideon took his men down to the river, where God said, "Everyone who laps with his tongue shall join you on one side, and everyone who kneels to drink shall join the other." Three hundred men lapped while the rest knelt to drink. (Judges 7:2-6)

God spoke to Gideon, announcing that he would utilize only the three hundred men who lapped at the stream to rescue them and give Midian into Gideon's hands. With all their provisions and trumpets, Gideon sent the Israelites, apart from the faithful, three hundred home. From a high point, Gideon gazed down at Midian's encampment below in the valley.

That night, God urged Gideon to venture down to the enemy's camp, reassuring him that it was already his. Despite any uncertainties, Gideon went down with his armor-bearer Purah to where the sentries were posted. Everywhere, Midian and Amalek forces stretched like a swarm of locusts, and their camels were too many to count.

As Gideon and Purah lurked, Gideon's timing was perfect because he overheard a man recounting his dream to a friend. The man said, "Last night I dreamed that a loaf of barley bread tumbled into the Midianite camp. It came to the tent and hit it so hard it collapsed. The tent fell!" His friend confidently replied, "This must be none other than the sword of Gideon son of Joash, the Israelite! God has turned Midian—the entire camp!—over to him."

When Gideon heard the dream and its interpretation, he fell to his knees in prayer to God. Blessed with newfound confidence, he rallied his Israelite forces, proclaiming, "Arise and conquer! God Himself has bestowed upon us the defeat of the Midianite army!"

Dividing his three hundred men into three companies, he bestowed upon each a trumpet and an empty jar with a torch inside. Leading by example, they approached the edge of the Midianite camp, waiting for the right moment to strike. As they prepared to attack, they united their voices in a mighty shout, echoing through the valley, "For God and for Gideon!" The startled Midianites leaped to their feet in terror as the three hundred trumpets blared, and the Israelites smashed the jars.

With each man brandishing a glorious torch in his left hand and a trumpet in his right, the Israelites declared, "A sword for God and for Gideon!" From all sides of the camp, they emerged, and the Midianites, seized with fear, scattered in every direction.

In the chaos, God Himself turned the Midianites against one another, and they fled in panic.

The Israelites united, summoning their warriors from all corners of Naphtali, Asher, and Manasseh to fight for their freedom against the oppressive Midianites. Encouraging the hill country of Ephraim to join them in their quest, Gideon sent messengers to rally the troops and orchestrated a surprise attack, capturing the fords of the Jordan at

Beth Barah. Triumphantly, they seized and executed the two Midianite commanders, Oreb (Raven) and Zeeb (Wolf), at Raven Rock and Wolf Winepress, respectively. Their victory fueled their pursuit of Midian, and they presented the slain commanders' heads to Gideon as proof of their success across the Jordan.

THANK GOD FOR A NEW MIND

The mind is incredibly powerful. Our thoughts shape our reality, dictate our emotions, and influence our actions. But Satan wants to hijack this power and steer it away from God's will. Whenever you try to move forward, whether it's towards a goal or overcoming a challenge, Satan will do his best to make you feel like you can't do it. He'll bombard you with negative thoughts and tell you that you're not capable or worthy. And if you're not careful, you'll start to believe him.

But that's where renewing your mind comes in. It's not just a spiritual buzzword but a powerful weapon that you can use to fight Satan's mind games. In Romans 12:2, we're instructed to "be transformed by the renewing of your mind." It means letting go of old patterns of thinking that don't serve us and replacing them with new ones that are aligned with God's truth.

So how do you renew your mind? Well, it starts with some self-awareness. Pay attention to the thoughts that enter your mind throughout the day, especially when you're faced with a challenge or setback. Are they positive or negative? Do they align with God's truth or with Satan's lies? Once you're aware of the patterns, you can start to challenge them.

The next step is to saturate your mind with God's truth. Reading the Bible, praying, and surrounding yourself with positive, faith-filled people are some ways you can do this. When you fill your mind with

God's word, you give him space to transform it and align it with his will.

Renewing your mind is not a one-time event

Our mind is one of the most powerful yet complex parts of our being. It's where our thoughts, beliefs, and emotions reside. Unfortunately, our mind can also be a breeding ground for negativity, anxiety, and self-doubt. It's why renewing our minds is not a one-time event but something that we need to do consistently. Renewing our mind is the discipline of replacing negative and untrue thoughts with positive and truthful ones. This enables us to take control of our thoughts and align them with God's truth. The process of renewing our minds is not easy, but it's worth it. It helps us experience freedom and power like never before.

Fill your mind with truth

In the battle against negativity and self-doubt, filling your mind with truth is a powerful weapon. Our minds are like sponges, absorbing the messages we hear and see. By actively choosing to fill your mind with positive, uplifting messages, you can shape your thoughts and beliefs. Reading the Bible or other inspiring books can help you see your worth and purpose. Listening to podcasts or sermons can challenge you to grow into your best self. As you saturate your mind with truth, you'll find that negative messages lose their power. Your mind will be stronger and clearer, and you'll be better equipped to stay resilient in the face of challenges.

Surround yourself with supportive people

It is important to recognize the impact that the people surrounding us have on our minds. Surrounding ourselves with supportive individuals can uplift our spirits and give us the confidence to pursue our dreams. Friends and loved ones can encourage and support us at times when life may seem challenging. It is equally important to connect with individuals who can advise and guide us as we navigate this journey. Sometimes, having a mentor or accountability partner can help us stay focused on our goals, remind us of our strengths, and challenge us to grow. On the other hand, individuals who consistently bring negativity and doubt into our lives can drain our mental energy, and we may need to distance ourselves from them. Therefore, it is essential to be mindful of the people we surround ourselves with, for our minds are affected by those around us.

Chapter Seven

Strategy #4 – I Will Stand Tall With Other Believers

*Therefore encourage one
another and build one an-
other up, just as you are doing.*
-1 Thessalonians 5:11 NIV

Deborah and Lucy had been friends since meeting at church five years ago, always supporting each other through thick and thin. They shared a special bond rooted in their mutual faith in Jesus Christ.

The two friends often discussed the importance of serving others as an act of love to honor God. They volunteered at their church, were members of their community food bank, and always walked in the annual Susan G. Komen Race for a Cure event.

One day, Deborah was going to meet Lucy for coffee when she had an accident. She veered off the road and into a swamp when a deer ran in front of her car. As water filled the car, Deborah knew she had to get out quickly. After opening the driver-side window, Deborah crawled out before her car sunk deeper into the swamp. Standing on the side of the road in disbelief, Deborah was wet, muddy, and in shock. She was also without her purse, which had her phone inside. Deborah felt hopeless.

Walking slowly toward the coffee house, Deborah noticed no one stopped to ask if she needed help. And since she was dirty, she was sure no one would stop for her, much less ask her if she was okay.

Fighting back tears as she walked, Deborah heard a car pull up behind her. At first, she was relieved, but those feelings turned to fear as she wondered if she would only be getting herself into more trouble. She said a quiet prayer, "Please, Lord, help me and protect me." When she turned around, she saw a familiar face pull up behind her; it was Lucy! Deborah felt like God sent her a blessing from heaven.

Lucy jumped out of the car and ran to her friend. She explained how she was on her way to the coffee shop when she saw her walking along the side of the road. The two friends embraced as Deborah started to cry. Deborah thanked God for bringing such a wonderful friend into her life. But Lucy quickly reminded Deborah of all the times she was there for her.

As the two women sat in Lucy's car waiting for the tow truck to arrive, they talked about how thankful they were for their beautiful friendship—built on their love of Jesus Christ and each other.

Deborah and Lucy have the kind of friendship Paul asked the believers in Thessalonica to have in 1 Thessalonians 5:11.

> *Therefore encourage one*
> *another and build one an-*
> *other up, just as you are do-*
> *ing.*

While I accepted that my cancer diagnosis was part of my journey, I made a conscious decision about how to deal with cancer. From the start, I decided that I wouldn't tell everyone in my life that I had cancer. I had no intention of introducing my cancer to everyone in my life. I didn't want to talk about cancer all the time. I didn't want the subject of cancer to invade my conversations or take up hours of my life that I could spend on other things.

I put cancer in its place.

So, I only told a handful of people. In addition to having a beautiful, supportive family, which includes my in-laws and spiritual parents, I have my own Deborahs and Lucys, who do everything in their power to serve, support and celebrate me daily. So, when I told them I had cancer, the first thing these people did was start praying for me. I am so blessed to have so many powerful prayer warriors on "Team Karen" who didn't mind going into battle with me.

I thank God for my family and friends.

Heavenly Father,

I bow before you in gratitude for the precious gift
of friendships. I am blessed beyond measure to have

friends who understand the importance of salvation and the call to serve others. It fills my heart with joy and comfort to know that there are those in my life who truly care about my well-being and seek to uplift me in your name. Father, thank you for the countless moments of laughter, support, and encouragement shared with these wonderful souls. May your love and grace continue to bind our hearts together in unity, today and always.

In Jesus' name, Amen.

THE BEAUTY OF FRIENDSHIPS

When life gets tough, having genuine friends by your side adds another layer of comfort. God wants us to have the kind of friendships where we can rely on others and be there for them when they need us. God's Word highlights what it means to be a true friend, including:

1. being there for each other through both the good and the bad times,

2. telling the truth (in a nice way) even when it's tough,

3. showing the kind of love that's talked about in 1 Corinthians 13, and

4. being ready to give up your life if necessary. (John 15:13)

Consider all the people you've called friends throughout your life. Take a moment to reflect on how many of them meet the expectations. Then, take another moment to reflect on which friends you know will or will not join you on the battlefield. Look at the list of expectations again and ask yourself the following questions.

1. During my friendship with this person, have we been there for each other during good times and bad?

2. Do my friends who follow Christ tell me the truth?

3. Are my Christian friends and I showing each other 1 Corinthians 13 kind of love?

4. Would I lay my life down for this friend, and would they do the same for me?

In addition, we need friends who help us and encourage us to obey God's Word. Sometimes, following God's will requires more courage than we can summon on our own. That's when the unwavering support of our Christian friends becomes invaluable. Without them, it's easy to fall into a state of indifference, not wanting to disobey God intentionally, yet too scared to take a leap of faith.

The encouragement we're called to give isn't mere flattery or shallow motivation. It's about empowering others with the courage and strength they need to tackle overwhelming tasks. We paint a grander picture of why their obedience matters in God's kingdom. We acknowledge that their obedience brings glory to God and holds eternal significance.

Does this mean you should only have Christian friends? No. Should you only talk to or be kind to other Christians? No. Don't shut yourself off from the world, and don't make people who don't have a relationship with Christ feel bad. Share your faith with both your Christian and non-Christian friends. Don't stop sharing what God is doing in your life. And look for opportunities to serve your friends and those who aren't yet friends.

Because here's the thing: if you only speak to other Christians, you won't be able to complete the assignment Jesus gave you, which is, to make other disciples of Christ. (Matthew 28:19-20)

LESSONS FROM SCRIPTURE: David and Jonathan

One of the Bible's most remarkable friendships is between David and Jonathan, which begins in 1 Samuel 18. After defeating Goliath, Saul decided to keep David by his side, not allowing him to return to his father. During this time, David and Jonathan formed a deep bond. Jonathan's love for David was as strong as his love for himself, resulting in a unique covenant relationship. Jonathan thought so much of David that he took off his coat and presented it to David, along with his entire uniform, including his sword, bow, and even his belt.

After Saul sent his death squad to Ramah to kill him, David returned to Jonathan with questions. "What have I done to make your father want to kill me?" While Jonathan did not know what David was talking about, he was determined to help his friend find answers. The two friends agreed that David would stay away during the New Moon festival. If Saul asked where David was, Jonathan would say David had returned home to Bethlehem for an annual sacrifice with his family. If Saul was okay with David's decision to go home, then they agreed David was safe. But if Saul got angry, Jonathan would know his father wanted to kill David. This plan meant Jonathan would have to lie to his father about David's whereabouts because David would be hiding in the field waiting to hear from Jonathan.

Jonathan was willing to go to great lengths for David because he loved him and because they made a covenant with each other that lasted as long as Jonathan was alive. Even when Jonathan discovered his father's intense jealousy towards David, he still stood by David. Jonathan never felt jealous that David would become the next king of Israel. Despite Saul's continual attacks on David, Jonathan asked David to treat his family with kindness and mercy, which David agreed to do.

There is no doubt that Jonathan and David shared a special bond. But their relationship held significant meaning in other areas.

Jonathan listened to David

When we think of listening, we often associate it with our ears and hearing. But in reality, listening is a function of the mind. The act of truly listening requires intentional focus and engagement, which is exactly what Jonathan demonstrated when he heard David speaking to Saul. Despite his own position as the king's son, Jonathan recognized David's worth and chose to listen and show him love and respect. This serves as a reminder to us all that listening is not just a passive act but rather an active and intentional choice that can lead to deeper understanding and meaningful relationships.

Jonathan showed David respect

In the biblical story of David and Jonathan, Jonathan's respect for David is made clear through his actions. Jonathan generously offers David his official garments and armor, which denotes more than just a friendly gesture. This act of respect indicates that Jonathan viewed David as his peer and held him in high esteem. Furthermore, by giving David his official garments and armor, Jonathan acknowledged that David would eventually take his place. The exchange between Jonathan and David underscores the importance of showing respect to others, regardless of their position or status. Respect is a crucial aspect of building healthy relationships.

Jonathan and David made plans

Jonathan and David were not just friends; they were partners in a plan. In a covenant agreement, they agreed that when David became king, Jonathan would be next in line for leadership. These plans spoke to the level of trust and commitment that they had towards each other. But their plans would not go unnoticed, especially by Saul, who would grow increasingly resentful of their bond. Despite the challenges they faced, Jonathan and David stayed true to their plans, cementing their legacy as having one of the best examples of friendship in the Bible.

THE BENEFITS OF UNITING WITH OTHER CHRISTIAN BELIEVERS

Are you surrounded by other Christian believers who are committed to the same goal as you? It can be easy for us to become isolated in our struggles and battles, but that does not have to be the case. The Bible speaks of the importance of uniting with others and bearing each other's burdens to achieve greater success in our spiritual journeys.

The Power of uniting together

There is great power in connecting with other believers who share your same goals. In 1 Thessalonians 5:11, we are called to "encourage one another and build each other up." By uniting together, we can provide support and motivation to those around us. We can remind each other of the truth in God's Word and cheer one another toward achieving our goals. When we come together, we become a body unified by faith, stronger than any individual could ever be alone (Hebrews 10:25).

Two people working together are much better than one

There is a special bond when two or more people come together for a common purpose; it creates an environment where we can both give and receive strength from each other. Proverbs 27:17 says, "As iron sharpens iron, so one person sharpens another." Iron sharpening iron implies that when two objects rub against each other for a long enough period, they will chip away at each other's flaws until what remains is perfect—in this case, purified faith (1 John 1:7).

Biblical friendships offer strength

It's not always easy, but having a community of supportive believers around you can provide strength and encouragement when your faith is tested. Proverbs 27:17 says, "As iron sharpens iron, so one person sharpens another." When you have friends walking with you toward the same goal, they can lift your spirit and remind you of God's promises even when things seem impossible. When surrounded by other believers with similar struggles, hopes, and dreams, we can come alongside each other in love and understanding as we strive for righteousness.

Ecclesiastes 4:9-12 says, "Two are better than one because they have a good return for their labor; if either of them falls down, one can help the other up... A cord of three strands is not quickly broken." This verse reminds us that although finding these kinds of relationships may be difficult, it is worth investing time and energy into creating them because they will bear fruit. And when disagreements arise or sin creeps in (as it inevitably does), we should unite as pure people set apart for God's plans (1 John 1:7).

Chapter Eight

Strategy #5 –
I Will Walk In
Victory

> *For everyone born of God*
> *overcomes the world. This is*
> *the victory that has over-*
> *come the world, even our*
> *faith*
> -1 John 5:4, NIV

D uring the 1996 Olympics, the US Gymnast Team could see the gold medal within their reach. Team USA had a commanding lead of 0.897 points in the last rotation. They had only one competition left - the vault.

Unfortunately, things were not going well for the team. Four athletes for the USA team still needed to stick the landing. When it was Keri Strug's turn, everyone knew that her two vaults could determine whether Team USA took home gold or silver.

When Keri landed awkwardly on her feet, her ankle buckled underneath her. The pain was written all over Strug's face. But she had another vault. She got up. Her coach said, "You can do it, Keri. I believe you can do it."

Limping as she walked, Keri positioned herself to try again. She kept her eyes on her coach to avoid thinking about her ankle. Keri found strength in her coach. Despite her limp, she walked over to the vault. She knew she needed to nail the landing.

Pain shot through her ankle as she limped towards the vault, but Keri pushed it away. Instead, she thought of her coach's encouraging words ringing in her ears: "You can do this!" Taking a deep breath, Keri sprinted forward with every ounce of strength left in her body. The crowd held their breath as they watched Keri soar gracefully into the air and stick the perfect landing. Their cheers erupted across the stadium. With her coach's encouragement, she completed a beautiful vault with a high enough score for the US to win the gold medal.

You can do this. You can do this. I keep hearing those powerful words ringing in my ears.

With every challenge you face, it's easy to feel discouraged and defeated. You may even wonder if all your efforts are worth it. But you and I don't need to worry about the outcome because Jesus has already declared our victory. Even though we will have struggles and hardships in this world, we can take heart knowing that He has overcome it all. It's time to adopt an attitude of perseverance and determination because we are on the winning team.

The Bible makes it clear that victory has already been granted to every believer:

> *"For everyone who has been born of God overcomes the world. And this is the victory that has overcome the world—our faith."* (1 John 5:4)

Yet, if we're being honest with each other, there have been times when we have lived defeated lives. We have allowed our circumstances to keep us from moving forward in God's plan for our lives. But the good news is that all of that can stop today.

WE ALREADY HAVE THE VICTORY

In Jesus Christ, you have it all. He has accomplished all. He has conquered all. He has generously given all. You already have every promise, every blessing, and every victory. I understand it may not seem or feel that way right now, but that's where the struggle lies. The battle isn't about trying to get something you lack; it's about choosing whether or not to tap into what already belongs to you in Christ Jesus.

Here's my question: Will you choose to accept God's everlasting truth despite your current temporary circumstances, or will you let today's outlook dictate your decision? This is the battle that often trips us up during challenging times.

Satan comes around and tries to mess with our minds. He'll attempt to fill our heads with negative thoughts, making us doubt if we'll ever make it out of this situation alive. He'll say that God can't help and that we're entirely on our own. If the enemy had his way, we'd start doubting God's promises, and our vision would get so clouded that we can't see the loving hand of Jesus trying to lead us out of the dark. Let me clarify something - the facts may be true at the time. You can have a pink slip that lets you know your job will be gone by the end of the month. If you are behind on your car payments, your car might get towed. And as much as I didn't want it, the lumps I felt in my body were still there, and I still had cancer.

But you know the saying, *Trouble don't last always.*

In 2 Corinthians 4:17-18, Paul reminds us that "these troubles and sufferings of ours are small and won't last very long. The troubles will soon be over, but the joys to come will last forever." In other translations, Paul refers to these troubles as "light" and "momentary." God doesn't want us to get hung up on every trial and tribulation to the point that we forget our faith in Him. You and I can put faith in action when nothing but God's Word and our hallelujah-any-how-born-again-spirit tell us to trust God's way.

And that, my friend, is the real battle. Satan wants you to believe his lies over God's truth. But I can assure you there is power in walking in victory no matter what troubles come your way.

LESSONS FROM SCRIPTURE: David and Goliath

Hebrews Chapter 11 introduces us to numerous faithful people from the Old Testament who trusted God wholeheartedly and displayed remarkable faith. David was among these remarkable saints.

David was successful because God was with him (1 Samuel 16:18). God's providential hand guided David. Even as a teenager, David wanted to bring glory to God. As a Spirit-led young man, David's footsteps were ordered to do the will of the Father.

Working part-time as part of King Saul's staff, David would go back and forth between Saul's house and his father, Jessie's home. But one day, Jessie asked David to take lunch to his brothers – Eliab, Abinadab, and Shammah. As members of Saul's army, they were camped at the valley of Elah (1 Sam 17:19).

Since Goliath was over nine feet tall, he is often referred to as a giant. Goliath represented the Philistine army. He challenged the army of Israel to send one man to fight him. If Israel succeeded in killing him, the Philistines would submit to Israel. But if Goliath won, the Israelites would become servants to the Philistines (1 Sam 17:8-9). Unfortunately, no one in the Jewish army, including King Saul, wanted to fight Goliath.

But in walks David. He asks the men: "What will be done for the man who kills that Philistine and removes this disgrace from Israel? Who is this uncircumcised Philistine that he should defy the armies of the living God?" (v. 26)

Although David was too young to join the army, he was prepared to go into battle. Saul sent for David (v. 31). David assured the king that he would care for Goliath. At first, Saul doubted that David could win. But he finally gave in and said, "All right, go ahead," he said, "and may the Lord be with you!" Little did Saul know, but God was already with David (See 1 Sam 18:12, 14, and 28). David surrendered to God's will for his life.

Saul didn't have the same faith David had in God, so he told David to wear his armor (vv. 38-39). Since Saul was a big man and David was a teenager, the armor didn't fit. David couldn't even walk. He removed Saul's armor and decided to go with what he knew – a staff, a slingshot, and five smooth stones. The sling was a shepherd's weapon that David knew how to use. But more importantly, David knew how to step out on faith.

When Goliath saw David, he laughed. "Am I a dog that you come at me with a stick?" he said (1 Sam 17:43). David wasn't intimidated. He trusted God to empower him and was willing to take a risk. He replied, "You come against me with sword and spear and javelin, but I come against you in the name of the Lord Almighty, the God of the armies of Israel, whom you have defied." (1 Sam 17:45)

David then took his slingshot and a stone, and with one well-placed shot, he brought down the giant. Goliath lay motionless in the field, and David became a hero. This story teaches us to step out on faith even when things seem impossible. We have no idea what lies beyond our comfort zone. We must be willing to take a risk, trust God's power and timing, and watch what can happen. "With man this is impossible, but with God all things are possible" (Matt 19:26).

It's easy to look at our present challenges and feel there's no way we could ever come out on top. But if we remember the story of David and Goliath, it's a reminder that God can do anything. We must be willing to step out on faith and courage in His name. With His power behind us, no challenge is too big.

Even when we feel inadequate or scared, He'll give us the strength to fight and get through.

Are you struggling to walk in victory as a believer? Have you ever felt that you lack the skills and knowledge to reach your goals, despite knowing that the Lord gives you everything you need to get by and succeed? You are not alone. For years I struggled to align God's word on victory in Christ Jesus to my life as a believer. No more. Over the years, I have learned to shout before the battle ends.

PRINCIPLES OF VICTORY

Walking in victory is a whole new ball game when you know you'll come out on top.

When we face trials or setbacks, it's easy to feel beaten down and discouraged. Especially when we lose our jobs, a relationship ends, or are buried in debt. We often forget that God's Word is a living, active weapon that can be used to defeat the enemy. However, remembering how it all ends can change our perspective on life.

Let's take financial struggles, for example. We can find solace in knowing that the most important debt has already been paid by the blood of Jesus (1 John 1:7). And when a relationship ends, we can remember that the Savior never leaves us or forsakes us (Hebrews 13:5). And when faced with a debilitating disease, we can remember by His stripes, we are healed (Isaiah 53:5).

Living a victorious life in Jesus isn't always easy, though. Sin, guilt, shame, and chaos can weigh us down. But there are ways to start walking in victory.

Prepare to fight God's way

Are you ready to take on life's battles? There's one crucial step before you start: Go to God! Building a strong relationship with Jesus is vital in knowing His plan for your life and preparing for each day, especially when life gets tough. Though we may feel we must fight alone, every battle is unique. If we're not prepared, we might miss the direction God wants us to take. After all, we have spiritual enemies that seek our downfall, so turning to God first is always the best course of action. Remember, our help comes directly from the Lord. He sits in Heavenly places and guides our every step through the Holy Spirit's wisdom in His Word.

Choose your weapons

How can we navigate our biggest struggles with God by our side? Well, Philippians 4:13 reminds us that through Christ, we can achieve anything. That's why walking with God daily is crucial, especially in the most challenging times. God always has our backs and will never falter in guiding us toward the right path. Ephesians 6:10-18 reinforces this idea, encouraging us to leverage every weapon in our spiritual toolbox. Armed with the authority of God and His Word, we can overcome anything life throws our way. Believers must focus on daily prayer, consistent Bible study, and a connection to the Holy Spirit to live in abundance. With God leading the charge, we can live victoriously, no matter what challenges arise.

Don't fear the enemy

Life is too short to live in fear. With 1 Peter 5:7 backing us up, we can trust God with all our cares because he genuinely cares for us. We're not in this alone; we have Jesus walking alongside us every step of the way. Don't let the enemy or the world intimidate you, the power of sin is no match for that of the blood of the Lamb, and Jesus' name carries immeasurable authority.

Be disciplined and self-controlled

As Christians, we must practice self-discipline and self-control by walking closely with God and embracing difficult times alongside Him. This implies adhering to His will and living in a way that glorifies Him as a new creation. Rather than surrendering to temptations, we must pursue what pleases and honors our Heavenly Father.

Everything will work out for your good

Romans 8:28-30 is such an empowering passage. It declares that God causes everything to work together for the good of those who love Him and are called according to His purpose. He predestined us to be like His Son, and when we respond to His calling, He justifies and glorifies us. Let your walk with Jesus be filled with confidence, knowing He is always with you every step of the way. On the cross, He already won the battle for us, so there's no need to fear tomorrow. With Jesus, you can have an abundant life full of faith and without fear. So go forth, and walk confidently with Christ, knowing you are never alone.

If you are looking for the ultimate weapon for your arsenal to win in life's battles, one key is studying the Bible. Spending time in God's word equips you to navigate any situation and make the right moves.

According to the Bible, Jesus claims the ultimate victory through faith (1 John 5:4). Understanding God's words on this matter is critical. Trusting in the absolute truth can lead us to triumphant living. Life becomes less stressful when you know how the story ends. God has equipped us to conquer battles and walk in victory.

Chapter Nine

Be Strong And Courageous

Have I not commanded
you? Be strong and coura-
geous. Do not be afraid; do
not be discouraged, for the
Lord your God will be with
you wherever you go.
-Joshua 1:9 NIV

After the death of Moses, God went to Joshua to tell him it was time to cross over the Jordan River into the Promised Land. The land of Canaan represents where God's people went after being set free from bondage in Egypt. Hebrews 3 describes Canaan as a place of rest and victory believers can enjoy. It also demonstrates that the deliverance from Egypt was preparation for the abundant life in Canaan.

As part of our Christian journey, we have been delivered from sin to experience abundant life. The wilderness was never God's intention as our final destination. Unfortunately, just like a whole generation of Israel perished in the wilderness, many Christians also remain spiritually dry and never fully live out God's abundant plan for their lives.

Still, the instructions were clear from God's mouth to Joshua's ears. Joshua was to lead the people to the land God promised them. Joshua was probably excited and a bit nervous, so God told him, "Be strong and courageous," and assured him he would be with him. God gives us the same beautiful promise to be with us no matter what we go through.

It's time to cross over from your wilderness experience into a place of rest and victory. Say goodbye to:

The fear and trembling that takes hold of your mind, body, and soul whenever you face trials, tribulations, challenges, or battles.

And say hello to:

A renewed mind and a peaceful resolve determined to step out on faith and stand on the promises of God no matter what challenges you face.

Welcome! Let's finish what we started.

STAY BATTLE-READY

You've come a long way to reach this point, and I'm proud of you. However, it's important not just to read this book but also to apply the truth of God's Word intentionally in your life. This is necessary for you to experience victory in spiritual warfare. Only then will you truly move closer to living the victorious life God wants you to live.

Aren't you tired of the enemy always pushing you around? Aren't you sick of being Satan's punching bag?

I know I was. And when I had time to think about all I would have to go through on my cancer journey, I knew I couldn't go into this battle in the same way I had in the past. Worry. Fear. Doubt. Shame. Guilt. *Did I say worry?* Depressed. Angry. Combative. *Did I say worry? I've done a lot of worrying during my battles.* Ready to fight people. Ready to quit. Ready to disappear. Ready to hide. Ready to run.

Until the day I said, "No more! Help me, God. I can't do this without you. I am no good on my own. I surrender all to you."

> *So give yourselves to God.*
> *Stand against the devil,*
> *and he will run away from*
> *you.* (James 4:7)

The devil never wanted me to reach that point. What point, you say? The point where I go into battle, giving everything to God. God wants you and me to be humble; the enemy wants us to be proud. God wants us to depend on Him when life gets tough; Satan wants us to depend on ourselves. So, one of the first things we must do to stay battle-ready is to understand that the world, our flesh, and Satan want to keep us away from God. Although Jesus delivered us from these enemies from our old life of sin, that doesn't stop Satan from trying to use any and everything to separate us from God. Let's examine each area.

The world (James 4:4). When James talks about the "world," he means a human society without God (James 4:7). In our society, the entire system opposes Christ and God. Developing a friendship with the world is likened to adultery. As believers, we are united with Christ

(Rom 7:4) and should remain loyal to Him. We are also told not to conform to the world's standards but instead to be transformed by renewing our minds (Rom 12:2).

The flesh (James 4:1, 5). When James talks about "the flesh," he means our old nature that tends to sin. When a sinner accepts Christ, they receive a new nature, but the old nature is not eradicated or transformed. As a result, there is an internal struggle: "For the sinful nature desires what is contrary to the Spirit, and the Spirit what is contrary to the sinful nature. They are in conflict with each other, so that you are not able to do what you want." (Gal 5:17). Choosing to live to please the old nature is essentially declaring war against God.

The Devil (James 4:6-7). The world fights the Father, the flesh fights the Holy Spirit, and the devil fights the Son of God. Pride is one of the enemy's weapons against the saint and the Savior. God wants us to rely on His grace, while the devil tries to inflate our egos, leading us to believe we can do everything ourselves. Remember when Peter cut off Malchus' ear with his sword during Jesus' arrest? Peter fell into the enemy's trap and acted impulsively.

Giving yourself to God and resisting the devil is your first line of defense.

Whether preparing for a battle, in a battle or coming out of a battle, it's important to stay battle-ready. You might be thinking, *"Am I just sitting around waiting for bad things to happen?"* No. You don't have to live on pins and needles, wondering when the next trial or tribulation will knock on your door. You can live a life of joy and peace but still be battle-ready by using the resources and tools God has graciously given us.

Aside from our day-to-day struggles, every believer must prepare for the return of Jesus Christ. As believers, we want to be ready. Paul gives us several warnings through his ministry in light of Christ's soon return. In Romans 13:14, he tells us to "put on" the Lord Jesus Christ, which means to become more like Him. Essentially, we should receive, through faith, all that Jesus is for our daily lives. Our growth is directly linked to the nourishment we consume. That's why God warns us against making provisions for the flesh. When we feed our fleshly desires, we are destined to fail. However, if we focus on feeding our inner being with the nourishing things of the Spirit, we are sure to succeed.

In addition to God's armor, let's look at what we have in our arsenal that we can use to feed our inner being and let our armor of light shine as part of our battle-ready plan.

Prayer

Prayer is a powerful tool that we often underestimate. I say this because I meet a lot of Christians who admit they don't pray as often as they should. For some believers, prayer at church on Sunday is all the praying they may do for an entire week. But prayer is our most powerful weapon. When we pray, we invite God to fight for us. Prayer is not just a one-way conversation; it's a conversation between us and our Heavenly Father. We can pour out our hearts to Him in prayer and listen for His voice. Prayer is not just a religious practice; it's a lifeline. When people ask me how I got through nearly 75 doctor appointments, six rounds of chemo, 30 radiation treatments, and surgery, I gladly say PRAYER.

God's Word

The Bible is not just a book; it's a spiritual weapon. We can use the Word of God to fight against the enemy. When we read the Bible and meditate on its truth, we fill our minds with the wisdom, promises, and the power of God. We can use Scripture to rebuke the devil, pray for healing, and seek guidance. The more we read and study God's Word, the better equipped we are to face life's battles.

Before cancer, I read the Bible or listened to an app. But during my treatments, my pastor encouraged me to increase my Bible intake practice by surrounding myself with God's Word. What does that mean? That means I would go to bed listening to Scriptures through my headphones besides what I was already doing. I would listen to Bible verses in my office, in the car, or during my chemo treatments. The calming effect of God's Word was all around me.

Praise and Worship

In one of my first prayers to God, I told Him I would attend church every Sunday during my cancer treatments if I had the strength. Praise is such a beautiful way to worship God, even in the midst of the storm. When we praise God, we declare who He is and what He has done for us. Since I had cancer during the pandemic, my church offered online services. But as long as I had strength in my body, I counted it as a privilege to go to church to worship in the sanctuary. Praising God helped to lift my spirits and changed my perspective. Praise can be expressed through worship, singing, dancing, or simply declaring God's goodness. But more importantly, it was a way for me to focus on God and His faithfulness.

Gratitude

I have always believed in the power of being grateful and showing gratitude. When we focus on what we're thankful for, we shift our focus away from our problems and onto God's blessings. When my son, Cole, had open-heart surgery at ten weeks old, he was in the intensive care unit with other babies and small children. Duke Hospital did a wonderful job of trying to create a colorful, playful environment in the children's rooms. During one of my visits to see Cole, I noticed a plush animal attached to his crib. I was so touched by the gesture that I purchased more of the same type of stuffed animals for the other children's beds. Gratitude opens our hearts to share more of

God's blessings. It's acknowledging God's provision and love in our lives. When we practice gratitude, we cultivate a heart of contentment, essential in spiritual warfare.

Serve

I could probably write a book about serving in God's Kingdom. Not because I know so much but because it is such a beautiful way to be Jesus's hands and feet in the world. Serving others is one of the most powerful ways of expressing our love for God and His people. When we serve others, we put our faith into action. And for me, serving helps me to focus on the needs of others instead of myself. It's a way of sharing God's love to the world. When we serve, we become less self-centered and more God-centered. Serving also helps us fight against the enemy's lies that tell us we're not good enough or have nothing to offer this world.

While I only share five examples, I encourage you to add more to your arsenal.

Remember, victory in spiritual warfare requires intentionally applying God's principles to our daily lives. It's not just about reading the Bible or going to church; it's about actively putting our faith into practice. Prayer, God's Word, praise, gratitude, and serving are powerful tools to prepare ourselves for the attacks on the horizon. But they are also ways to protect ourselves from the enemy and experience the abundant life God has promised us.

GO ON THE OFFENSIVE

How can you build your spiritual muscles in preparation for the battles you may face? The best way I know how to use the weapons in my arsenal in my daily life is through spiritual discipline. Christian spiritual disciplines are the God-ordained ways in Scripture to come before Him, experience Him, and become more like Christ. And my faith is much stronger when I intentionally focus on these practices personally and with other believers. Throughout history, we can find where God's people have embraced these habits of devotion and experiential Christianity.

To grow spiritually, different practices can help. Some are inward disciplines like Bible study, prayer, meditation, and fasting. Then there are outward practices like service and evangelism. Corporate practices include worship and stewardship. Are there more? Yes. Please research and find others to add to this list. Ultimately, spiritual disciplines must focus on a common goal: to foster spiritual growth and deepen our relationship with God.

The spiritual disciplines I focus on and study for the purpose of building my faith are Bible study, prayer, worship, evangelism, serving, stewardship, fasting, biblical meditation, journaling, and learning.

The spiritual disciplines help us to understand, love, and trust God. When we practice them regularly, they become holy habits that shape who we are and how we act. These habits make it easier for us to live out our identities in Christ. The choices we make every day create our habits, and our habits help to shape our character. Our character, in turn, influences our decisions, especially when faced with tough times, temptations, or battles. This is how mature believers, on the path of growth, reveal their inner beauty through their godly actions.

Let me be clear about one thing. Spiritual growth occurs from the inside out, not the other way around. It's more about the process of inner transformation than following external routines. This means our practices aren't magical, nor should we expect others to engage in the same disciplines. In the season you are in right now, you might need to focus on prayer, while I may need to strengthen my spiritual discipline related to worship. Bottom line: your walk with God must be a matter of the heart. Simply knowing God won't be enough. It's important to have a strong, whole-hearted commitment to loving and honoring God. If your commitment is only half-hearted, you'll soon grow tired or practice spiritual disciplines inconsistently.

So, if you want to focus on building or improving your spiritual disciplines to build your faith, here are a few things you may want to give up.

Give up your time

You must put in the time and effort to see real progress in your spiritual growth. Building or improving your spiritual discipline can't be done simply by wishing for it - you must commit to the process. It's easy to get distracted by life's many daily obligations and demands. Still, dedicated believers know that making time for their spiritual growth is crucial. Whether carving out a little extra time in the morning for prayer and meditation or spending a few more minutes with the Bible each day, investing in your spiritual growth is always a wise choice. So, if you want to strengthen your faith, it's time to give up some of your precious time and make a conscious effort to nurture your spiritual growth.

Give up needless distractions

If you're serious about strengthening your faith, it's time to buckle down and focus on your spiritual disciplines. That means cutting out any unnecessary distractions that may be hindering your progress. Whether mindlessly scrolling through social media for hours or binge-watching your favorite series on Netflix, these distractions can slow your spiritual growth. Instead, prioritize quiet time for prayer, meditation, and reading. It may not be easy initially, but the rewards of a stronger walk with Christ are well worth the effort. So why not take the necessary steps to strengthen your faith and give up those needless distractions?

Give up the impossible idea of being perfect

Let's face it, we all like to think that we've got it together when it comes to our spiritual lives. We set ambitious goals for ourselves regarding our prayer life, Bible study, and church attendance, convinced that we will execute them perfectly. But the truth is, we're human. We'll slip up, make mistakes, and miss a day in our daily devotions. And when that happens, it's easy to feel discouraged or like a failure. But here's the thing - that's not what building spiritual disciplines is all about. It's not about being perfect but about making a conscious effort to grow in your faith and trust in God. So, if you stumble, don't be too hard on yourself. Talk to God about it and ask for His help. Then dust yourself off and keep moving forward. Your faith walk is a marathon, not a sprint.

You set yourself up for an incredible transformation as you practice spiritual disciplines. Through consistent and intentional effort, you will begin to see the world through the lens of the Bible, which will, in turn, impact your actions and thoughts. This transformation won't happen overnight but day by day. But it all starts with a willingness to dive in and make an effort. I encourage you to embrace the challenge of practicing spiritual disciplines with eagerness and expectation, knowing that your heart and life will be forever changed. I know mine has been.

ON THE DEFENSIVE

I realize that we've spent quite a bit of time on the offensive and how to prepare for possible trials and tribulations, and you might be saying, "Help! I'm in a battle right now. What am I supposed to do? Here are three things you can do:

1. Go to God in prayer and ask Him for help and guidance.

2. Worship the Lord through fear and uncertainty.

3. Trust in God's guidance, then take a step forward in faith.

It's easy to feel overwhelmed when facing battles in life. But it's important to remember that God will meet you on the battlefield no matter what you're going through. Whether you're just starting to build your spiritual disciplines or you've been strengthening them for years, God will meet you right where you are. Embrace the challenges and trust in His plan. With God on your side, you can face any battle that comes your way.

Chapter Ten

Victory Is Ours

But thanks be to God, who
gives us the victory through
our Lord Jesus Christ.
-1 Corinthians 15:57 NIV

Remember our global traveler from Chapter Six of this book? The global traveler was left alone on a deserted island as part of an extreme vacation. We imagined what the global traveler must have felt and thought alone on the island. We imagined hopelessness, self-doubt, fear, and desperation. Let's look at the story again through a different lens.

The global traveler sat on the beach, looking over the vast ocean. Unsure of what to do next, he started to pray:

Dear God,

Thank you, God, for bringing me to this beautiful place.
I'm not sure what to do next, but I feel your peace here.
You are Jehovah Shalom, who spoke to the wind and
the waves, calming them with just one word. Only you
can bring peace to my heart, mind, and soul. As I sit
here, worries try to invade my mind. Please forgive me
for entertaining thoughts of fear, worry, and doubt,
and grant me the grace of your peace. Thank you for
making your peace available to me. Jehovah Shalom,
I speak shalom into my mind and actions right now.
Show yourself to me and reveal to me what I need to do
now, in the name of Jesus. Amen.

As you open your eyes, you feel better than before. As you look around the island to see what materials you can use to build a shelter, you see your guide returning. He's not alone. You see at least three people with him.

Now, imagine you are the global traveler. What kind of people do you hope are in the boat?

Maybe you hope for someone with vision. You need someone to help you look around the island to see the big picture. A few minutes ago, you were thinking about stacking a few sticks together in hopes that you could protect yourself from the sun and rain. But maybe your vision isn't great enough. Perhaps someone in the boat can help you see yourself in a bigger shelter where you can rest. It sounds like what you need is a visionary.

Next, you hope someone in the boat can encourage you. When you signed up for this adventure, you had no idea it would be so lonely and discouraging. You think about how nice it would be to talk to someone positive and full of wisdom. It would be nice to laugh again. Perhaps even someone who has been in a place like this before.

Finally, it would be nice to have a guide on this island. You didn't even attempt to go deeper into the island because the trees and brush looked too thick. It would really help if they had a knife or a machete so they could help you cut a path through the island.

Feelings of defeat start to fade when your rescuer shows up. Your loneliness subsides because you have companionship. Your misery diminishes because you have a vision. Your mental fog begins to lift because you have direction. You are not meant to stay here; you're just a pilgrim passing through. Hebrews 13:14 makes it plain, "For this world is not our home; we are looking forward to our everlasting home in heaven." But while we're here, we have comfort knowing we can look to the hills for help (Psalm 121:1-2).

Because of the comfort of the Father, the Son, and the Holy Spirit, you feel so much better.

And guess what? You're still on a deserted island. Your surroundings haven't changed, but you have. You changed because you saw victory within reach. You changed because you remembered when Jesus said, "In the world you will have tribulation. But take heart; I have overcome the world." (John 16:33). You changed because your hope was restored.

We can continue on this journey because of what Jesus did for you and me, knowing we are overcomers.

MARCHING ORDERS

No matter what battles you face in life, remember that God is always with you on the battlefield. It might feel like you're alone, but rest assured that He is by your side, full of the strength and courage you may lack. So instead of feeling defeated and powerless, hold your head high and know you can overcome your challenges with His help. With the right attitude and unwavering faith, you can conquer any obstacle that comes your way.

And, because of your love for Jesus, I hope you'll do one more thing - Share your story.

For many Christians, the church is limited to Sunday morning worship with little to no regard for what goes on during the rest of the week. Fewer than 20 percent of the people in the average church have shared their faith with others in the past year. As a result, over 80 percent of Christians deny Jesus by never talking about Him to others. A Christian who never shares the gospel of Jesus Christ is just as guilty of the same sin of silence as Peter in denying having known Christ.

Tell someone about your struggles in hopes of helping them reach the other side of worry, guilt, shame, and brokenness. Tell someone about the saving grace of our Lord and Savior, Jesus Christ. Talk about the day you gave your life to Christ. Describe how you felt the day He touched your heart. Talk about the moments you used God's strength to overcome turbulent times. Let them know that life with Christ comes complete with a Heavenly Father and a Comforter and Guide in the form of the Holy Spirit.

And while you may not be able to tell everybody, you certainly can tell somebody.

In the heat of a battle, it is easy to lose focus on what truly matters. That's why having a solid foundation of faith is so important. When we find ourselves in the midst of chaos, we can turn to God's word for guidance and strength. By calling on the name of Jesus, we open ourselves up to a better path forward. It's not always easy, but by keeping our faith strong, we can trust in His plan for us. So the next time you feel overwhelmed, remember to lean on your faith and trust that Jesus will answer your call. God's strength and power can help you come out better than before.

Final Word

I hope this book has inspired you and that you walk away with a new outlook on facing the battles in your life.

During my cancer battle, I consciously focused on my faith walk in the weeks following my diagnosis. Not knowing what the future would hold, I let my faith in God guide me. Not only did I want people to see my trust in God, but I also wanted to walk by faith, not by sight.

Whenever someone asked me how I was doing or about how I was handling my treatments, I would say, 'I'm walking in victory.'

And that's how I made it through every chemo treatment, surgery, and radiation appointment. I walked believing I would see victory every step of the way.

My cancer journey has been peaceful. Throughout my year-long treatment, God performed miracle after miracle. I share more about my cancer story on my **blog** at www.karenbrowntyson.com

On Wednesday, October 26, 2022, I went to the UNC Rex Cancer Center for my last cancer treatment.

I am officially cancer free! And I'm giving God all the glory.

About the Author

Karen Brown Tyson is an acclaimed author who has written books like *"Time to Refresh: A 21-Day Devotional to Renew Your Mind After Being Laid Off, Fired or Sidelined"* and *"Time to Reset: A 21-Day Devotional to Renew Your Mind After Being Sidelined, Disappointed or Knocked Off Course."* Her first book, *Time to Refresh*, was named a 2019 Finalist in the Religion: Christian Inspirational Category of the 2019 Best Book Awards.

She has a Bachelor of Arts degree in English from West Virginia University and a Master of Arts in English from National University. In addition, Karen has a Master of Arts degree in Christian Ministry and postgraduate certificates in Christian Leadership, Theological Studies, and Biblical Studies from Liberty University Rawlings School of Divinity. Her ministry concentration focuses on the expository teaching of the Word of God in spiritual discipline, discipleship, leadership, apologetics, and New Testament theology.

Karen serves to advance God's kingdom in various ways, including her most recent assignments with the Deacon's Wives, Women, Evangelism, Social Media and Helps ministries at Elevation Baptist Church. Karen also serves as the Dean of the Elevation Bible Institute, teaching courses on spiritual discipline, evangelism, discipleship, and Christian apologetics.

Karen is a Jerry Jenkins Christian Writer's Guild Apprentice Program graduate. As a writer, she has developed several Christian ministry tools and training materials for her local church.

When she is not writing or studying, Karen loves spending time with her husband of 28 years, Kelvin, and their son, Cole. They live in North Carolina.

Acknowledgements

I couldn't have written this book without the help and support of so many amazing and loving people. I'm incredibly grateful for the support I've received from my family, friends, and mentors. I can't thank God enough for continuously blessing me and answering my prayers. And where do I even begin with my husband, Kelvin? He's my true love and my best friend for life. And my incredible son, Cole? He's simply the best son a mother could ever want.

I'm grateful for my mother, Edna Brown, and my aunt, Jeffie Jackson, who lived to be 91 and 92 years old. Although they both went home to be with the Lord while I was writing this book, I am forever grateful for their love and support. I'm thankful to my brother, James Brown, for always lifting me on his shoulders to celebrate me.

I thank God for my entire family in Savannah, Georgia. To my cousins Cheryl Barnes, Charlene Daniels, and Donald Lambert, thank you for always encouraging me.

I thank God for my anointed niece, Payton, and my sister-in-love Robinette, for your prayers that helped this book cross the finish line. And God has blessed me with a brother and sister-in-love, Karsten and Pam, who will drop everything to help me; I love you both. And to my late mother-in-love, Beverly Tyson, thank you for your gift of love.

I'm grateful to my spiritual parents, Pastor T.L. and Elder Rebecca Carmichael. Thank you for being with me through every hill and valley. I appreciate your prayers, encouragement, and for showing me the amazing truth of God's word.

I'm grateful to my Ohio and North Carolina cousins – Traci Higgins, "Little Bernice," Natalie Shaw, and Nicole Mason for always supporting and encouraging me. And to Amy Lou Anderson, thank you for being such an awesome cheerleader and prayer warrior!

Speaking of prayer warriors, I am grateful for the entire Levett Family Prayer Circle. Your powerful prayers helped me get through every cancer treatment and doctor's appointment. And to Pat, thank you for your advice and encouragement on my journey. Your beautiful text messages meant more to me than you will ever know.

And I wouldn't even have access to the Levett Family Prayer Circle without Lucy and Willie Levett. I know you both are Kelvin's childhood friends, but I feel like I have known you my whole life. Probably because of all the love and support you have shown me since we met more than 20 years ago. I am grateful to you both. And Lucy, you are the best sister in Christ I could have ever asked for!

Speaking of true sisters in Christ, I'm grateful to Robin Byrd for always supporting and encouraging me. And, to Deborah Cearnel, I cannot thank you enough for your love. From our cycling days when we just had to figure it out for ourselves to the unknown journey through cancer, you aren't afraid of any challenge, and I love you for that. To Jeffrey Cearnel, thank you for calling me with words of encouragement and for going to Cole's swim meets when I was too weak to stand.

I thank God for Beverly and Kevin Armwood for always being right there to help. I appreciate your faithful friendship, love, and courage to step on the battlefield with me.

I'm grateful to Dia Cox Selby for doing more than taking care of my hair. Thank you for your prayers and love.

I'm grateful to Christopher Hunt for the advice you shared with my husband and the prayers and encouragement you extended to me.

I'm grateful to Cara McLauchlan for being a prayer warrior and for your years of friendship, love, and support.

Thank you, Denise Campana, Joyce Ward, Sonja Ellis Watson, and Terry Bradley Dunn, for reading my books and always offering encouraging words. And to my Sam Brown, Inc. Healthcare Communications family, thank you for taking a moment to celebrate my victory after the battle.

I'm grateful to Justina Parker and Vivian Green for sharing your testimonies about their breast cancer journeys. I learned valuable information that helped me more than you know.

I'm grateful to all my doctors, nurses, coordinators, physician assistants, radiology technicians, physical therapists, receptionists, and parking valets at the UNC Rex Cancer Center. In addition to my treatments, your kindness was just the medicine I needed.

I'm grateful to the beautiful women of Elevation Baptist Church, who show me so much love by purchasing my books. Finally, I am thankful for the many people I haven't explicitly mentioned who pray for and motivate me.

Leave a Review

If you enjoyed this book, please consider sharing the message with others.
Mention the book in a Facebook post, Pinterest pin, a blog post, or upload a picture to Instagram.
Recommend the book to people in your small group study, book club, and classes.
Pick up a copy for someone you know whom the book would inspire.
Share a book review on Amazon.

Visit my website at www.karenbrowntyson.com to learn more about my Time to Grow in Grace series and my next book, **Time to Rejoice: A 21-Day Devotional to Renew Your Mind After Being Knocked Off Course, Let Down or Broken.** Scheduled for release in 2024.

Reflective
Questions

Chapter 1

1. Ephesians 6:12 reminds us that our battle is not against the people around us, *For we are not fighting against people made of flesh and blood but against* (fill in the blank):

   _____

2. What do you think Satan desires to gain by deceiving us?

3. Everyone didn't like Jesus. Everyone didn't accept Jesus. As a result, Jesus tells His disciples, "If the world hates you, keep in mind that it hated me first." (John 15:18).

   - How does this make you feel?

   - How do you deal with a world that doesn't always accept Christian beliefs?

4. Our faith isn't tested because God is clueless about how much or what kind of faith we possess. It's put to the test because *we often have no idea ourselves.*

   - When was the last time your faith was tested?

   - What did you learn about yourself during your last test?

5. Why do you think Barak was reluctant to go to war without Deborah?

  ○ What surprised you most about the story of Barak and Deborah?

Chapter 2

1. In 1 King 18, what did people witness Elijah doing at Mount Carmel?

2. Why did Elijah decide to run in 1 Kings 19?

   ○ In your own words, describe how Elijah must have felt.

   ○ Describe a time when you wanted to run away from your problems.

3. Why do you think God asked Elijah, "What are you doing here?" (1 Kings 19:9)

   ○ What did God do after He told Elijah to "Go out and stand on the mountain" (1 Kings 19:11)

   ○ What point do you think God was trying to make in 1 Kings 19: 11-13?

4. The author of this book talks about feeling discouraged after her cancer diagnosis.

   ○ Have you ever felt discouraged after receiving unexpected news?

○ How did you respond?

5. Mark 2:3-5 reminds us of a group of men desperate to have their friend healed by Jesus.

○ What did Jesus say and do?

Chapter 3

1. According to this chapter, no one can escape life's (fill in the blank) _____

2. What are Peter's instructions in 1 Peter 5:6-11?

3. What happened when Naaman went to Elisha's house?

   ○ Why do you think Naaman got angry with Elisha?

   ○ How did Elisha deliver his message to Naaman?

4. What were Elisha's instructions to Naaman?

   ○ What did Naaman do when he initially heard Elisha's instructions?

   ○ Who spoke to Naaman to get him to change his mind?

5. What happened to Naaman after he came out of the Jordan River?

Chapter 4

1. In talking about the armor of God, who does Paul use as a model?

2. To stand strong against the enemy's attacks, we must wear (fill in the blank) _____ like a shield to protect our hearts.

3. Reflect on the times you had to put on the armor of God.

    ○ How did you use truth like a belt?

    ○ When did you have to use the sword of the Spirit?

4. What are your favorite parts of God's armor?

5. What is the significance of the prayer in Ephesians 6:18?

6. What did you think about the devil trying to tempt Jesus?

    ○ Reflect on when Satan tried to tempt you, but you didn't fall for it.

Chapter 5

1. What caused King Jehoshaphat to pray?

   ◦ Describe how you think King Jehoshaphat felt before he prayed.

   ◦ How do you deal with battles in your life?

   ◦ Reflect on a time when you prayed to avoid trouble in your life.

2. What message did Jahaziel deliver to everyone?

3. What did King Jehoshaphat encourage the people to do?

4. When the people of Judah looked over the hill, what did they see?

5. What did King Jehoshaphat and his people find when they approached the battlefield?

   ◦ What did everyone do on the fourth day when they reached the Valley of Blessing (Beracah)

   ◦ Reflect on a time when you found blessings after a battle.

Chapter 6

1. True dedication to God involves us giving Him our (fill in the blank) _____

2. Why do you think it's important to renew your mind constantly?

    ◦ What's one way you can renew your mind?

    ◦ Why do you think God doesn't automatically renew our minds Himself?

3. Give an example of how your mind has been renewed through God's Word.

    ◦ What beliefs did you have that were changed by studying God's Word?

4. Why do you think Gideon was hesitant when approached by God?

    ◦ Reflect on a time when you questioned God's assignment for your life.

    ◦ How did you renew your mind to accept your assignment?

5. After Gideon told God he was the "runt" of this family, what did God say to Gideon?

Chapter 7

1. This chapter starts with the story of two Christian friends, Deborah and Lucy. Take a moment to reflect on your friendships.

   - Do you have any close friends at your church?

   - What types of things do you do to serve your friends?

   - What do your friends do to serve you?

2. Why do you think Jonathan continued his friendship with David after discovering how Saul felt about him?

   - Why was Saul after David?

   - Where did the two friends agree David would hide until he heard from Jonathan?

3. Describe how David and Jonathan must have felt knowing Saul wanted David dead.

4. If you were fighting a battle, which friend would you call?

5. Do you have non-Christian friends?

- How often do you share what God is doing in your life with these friends?

- How often do you pray for these friends?

Chapter 8

1. According to 1 Samuel 16:18, why was David successful?

2. How did David end up visiting the battlefield?

   ◦ When David heard about Goliath, what did he ask the men?

   ◦ How tall was Goliath?

   ◦ What did Saul do when he heard David was asking questions?

3. What did Goliath say when he saw David? How would you describe Goliath's attitude toward David?

4. Why do you think Saul offered David his armor?

   ◦ How did David go into battle?

   ◦ Why do you think David chose the weapons he did to fight Goliath?

5. What do you think the story of David and Goliath should teach us?

6. How do you deal with the giants in your life?

Chapter 9

1. After the death of Moses, what did God say to Joshua?

2. What does James 4:7 tell us to do?

    ○ How often do you apply this Scripture to your life?

    ○ Describe a time when you applied this Scripture.

3. What more can you do to prepare for and deal with the battles in your life?

4. What are spiritual disciplines?

    ○ How can spiritual disciplines help you deal with trials in life?

    ○ Which spiritual disciplines do you currently practice?

    ○ Are there any spiritual disciplines you want to get better at practicing?

5. If you want to focus on building or improving your spiritual disciplines to build your faith, what will you have to give up?

Chapter 10

1. What did you learn from the story about the global traveler?

2. After reading this book, what did you learn about God?

    ○ What did you learn about yourself?

    ○ What's one thing that you will add to your battle plan when facing trials and tribulations?

3. Do you understand the importance of sharing your story of faith with others who don't know Christ as their Lord and Savior?

    ○ Identify at least one person who you can share your faith with.

    ○ Identify someone you can invite to your church.

    ○ Identify someone you can serve and use the opportunity to tell that person about Christ.

    ○ How can you put the love of Christ on display?

4. What will you remember about God's power the next time

you face an obstacle?

5. Identify at least one way you are better after your most recent battle.

Sources

Chapter 1

Tony Evans Bible Commentary. Copyright © 2019 by Holman Bible Publishers

Chapter 2

Guzik, David. "Study Guide for 1 Kings 18,19." Blue Letter Bible. 7 Jul, 2006. Web. 9 Jul, 2018.

Tony Evans Bible Commentary. Copyright © 2019 by Holman Bible Publishers

Chapter 3

Guzik, David. "Study Guide for 2 Kings 5." Blue Letter Bible. 21 Feb, 2017.

Tony Evans Bible Commentary. Copyright © 2019 by Holman Bible Publishers

Chapter 4

Guzik, David. "Study Guide for Ephesians 6." Blue Letter Bible. 21 Feb, 2017.

Hoehner, Harold W. Ephesians: An Exegetical Commentary, 16160-16161.

MacDonald, Margaret Y. Sacra Pagina: Colossians and Ephesians. © 2000, © 2008 with updated bibliography by Order of Saint Benedict, Collegeville, Minnesota. All rights reserved.

Tony Evans Bible Commentary. Copyright © 2019 by Holman Bible Publishers

Chapter 5

Guzik, David. "Study Guide for 2 Chronicles 20." Blue Letter Bible. 21 Feb, 2017.

The Inspiring Life of George Müller. https://guideposts.org/insp iring-stories/the-inspiring-life-of-george-muller

Tony Evans Bible Commentary. Copyright © 2019 by Holman Bible Publishers

Chapter 6

Tony Evans Bible Commentary. Copyright © 2019 by Holman Bible Publishers

Wiersbe, Warren. *Be Right: How to Be Right With God, Yourself and Others.* © 1977 by David C. Cook

Chapter 7

Tony Evans Bible Commentary. Copyright © 2019 by Holman Bible Publishers

Wiersbe, Warren. *Be Successful: Attaining Wealth Money Can't Buy.* © 2021 by David C. Cook

Chapter 8

Tony Evans Bible Commentary. Copyright © 2019 by Holman Bible Publishers

Kerri Strug: The gymnast who battled through pain for a taste of Olympic glory.

Chapter 9

Tony Evans Bible Commentary. Copyright © 2019 by Holman Bible Publishers

Wiersbe, Warren. *Be Mature: Growing Up in Christ.* © 1978 by David C. Cook

Whitney, Donald S. Spiritual Disciplines for the Christian Life with Bonus Content (Pilgrimage Growth Guide) (p. 185). NavPress. Kindle Edition.

Chapter 10

Tony Evans Bible Commentary. Copyright © 2019 by Holman Bible Publishers

My Notes

www.ingramcontent.com/pod-product-compliance
Lightning Source LLC
Chambersburg PA
CBHW070723130626
46553CB00005B/2117